WRITINGS ON BALLET AND MUSIC

Titles in Print
The Origins of the Bolero School, edited by Javier Suarez-Pajares and Xoán M. Carreira
Carlo Blasis in Russia by Elizabeth Souritz, with preface by Selma Jeanne Cohen
Of, By, and For the People: Dancing on the Left in the 1930s, edited by Lynn
    Garafola
Dancing in Montreal: Seeds of a Choreographic History by Iro Tembeck
The Making of a Choreographer: Ninette de Valois and "Bar aux Folies-Bergère"
    by Beth Genné
Ned Wayburn and the Dance Routine: From Vaudeville to the "Ziegfeld Follies"
    by Barbara Stratyner
Rethinking the Sylph: New Perspectives on the Romantic Ballet, edited by Lynn
    Garafola (available from the University Press of New England)
Dance for Export: Cultural Diplomacy and the Cold War by Naima
    Prevots, with introduction by Eric Foner (available from the University Press of
    New England)
José Limón: An Unfinished Memoir, edited by Lynn Garafola, with introduction by
    Deborah Jowitt, foreword by Carla Maxwell, and afterword by Norton Owen
    (available from the University Press of New England)
Dancing Desires: Choreographing Sexualities on and off the Stage, edited by Jane
    C. Desmond
Dancing Many Drums: Excavations in African American Dance, edited by Thomas
    F. DeFrantz
Writings on Ballet and Music by Fedor Lopukhov, edited and with an introduction
    by Stephanie Jordan, translations by Dorinda Offord

A STUDIES IN DANCE HISTORY BOOK

WRITINGS ON BALLET AND MUSIC

FEDOR LOPUKHOV

EDITED AND WITH AN INTRODUCTION BY

STEPHANIE JORDAN

TRANSLATIONS BY

DORINDA OFFORD

THE UNIVERSITY OF WISCONSIN PRESS

The University of Wisconsin Press
1930 Monroe Street
Madison, Wisconsin 53711

www.wisc.edu/wisconsinpress/

3 Henrietta Street
London WC2E 8LU, England

5   4   3   2   1

Printed in the United States of America

Library of Congress Cataloging-in-Publication Data
Lopukhov, Fedor Vasilevich, 1886–1973.
Writings on ballet and music / Fedor Lopukhov;
edited and with an introduction by Stephanie Jordan;
translations by Dorinda Offord.
p. cm.
Translated from Russian. Includes
bibliographical references (p.) and index.
ISBN 0-299-18270-3 (cloth: alk. paper)
ISBN 0-299-18274-6 (pbk.: alk. paper)
1. Ballet. 2. Modern dance. 3. Music and dance.
I. Jordan, Stephanie. II. Title.
GV1787 .L63   2002
792.8—dc21   2002002339

5765628

Contents

Preface

Perhaps the most important aspects of any book are its tales for the future, its suggestions of further avenues for research. Certainly, the idea for a book of translated theoretical writings by the Russian choreographer Fedor Lopukhov was prompted by my own work, *Moving Music: Dialogues with Music in Twentieth-Century Ballet* (2000). My introductory survey in that book could not fail to include some kind of reference to this enigmatic figure known in the West almost exclusively for his *Dance Symphony* of 1923 and for his influence on the young George Balanchine. The topic begged for more than a mere summary, a glimpse of Lopukhov's achievement. References in the literature to Lopukhov's 1925 treatise *The Ballet Master and His Art* clearly indicate the importance of his position in the development of nonnarrative, structurally sophisticated dance, as well as of a theory of relations with music. This was sufficient to provoke me to explore Lopukhov further, particularly given the incentive of Elizabeth Souritz's account of Lopukhov's work in her book *Soviet Choreographers in the 1920s*. Soon, after a cursory examination of Lopukhov's writings, I realized that a book of translations was the most appropriate way to advance recognition of his work by an English-speaking audience. After all, here was a detailed manifesto that would help to rectify the dearth of primary sources, and theoretical sources at that, in dance: a rare dance treatise of the early twentieth century that includes precise reference to the movement content of the nineteenth-century classics. I have also been inspired by the rapidly developing field of studies that link music and dance—witness the spate of recent dissertations, articles, and books, not to mention conference panels on the subject—and by the need to develop the history of relations between these two media. The writings are an invaluable source to those involved in musical-choreographic studies.

The translations, which include selections from both *The Ballet Master and His Art* and the 1972 *Choreographic Revelations,* speak for themselves. However, my introductory material and annotations are intended to illuminate points raised in the writings, as well as to contextualize them within dance history and, more specifically, within Russian culture and Lopukhov's own career. This material should be considered preliminary Lopukhov commentary. I have relied mainly on sources in English, the chief exceptions to this being those chapters from the two Lopukhov books mentioned that have not been translated here and also his autobiography, *Sixty Years in Ballet,* and *Fedor Lopukhov* by Galina Dobrovolskaya, the most extensive writing on the choreographer to date. My translator, Dorinda Offord, summarized and translated sections of these writings that had particular relevance to my focus. An in-depth perusal of the wider range of Russian sources on Lopukhov is certainly needed, and it is hoped that this volume will prompt further work and dialogue with Russian material. It, too, has tales for the future. With this in mind, I have included the full list of chapter titles for the books from which the translations have been selected (a summary of chapter content in the case of *The Ballet Master and His Art*), as well as a chronology of Lopukhov's ballets. The bibliography will also lead potential scholars to further source material.

My transliteration procedures are driven as much by the vision of future research projects as by the need to be accessible. I have opted for easily readable Russian within the body of my text, using the conventional forms of names of well-known figures. However, in references, I have used the form of transliteration that is easiest to turn into Russian script as an aid to scholars who might wish to access the sources in Russian. In all such matters I have been guided by Dorinda Offord. To her, first, my thanks, for being an inspirational collaborator, from the initial stages of summarizing Lopukhov's writings—which prompted the acceptance of my proposal by the board of Studies in Dance History—through the translation phase, to the search for material in Russian sources that would further illuminate the translated texts and demonstrate their position within Lopukhov's work. I could not have wished for a finer translator or a more lively mind with whom to debate the more obscure subtleties of Lopukhov's meaning. Dorinda's approach was flexible but also graciously firm on those occasions when our Russian author did not say what we wanted him to say. I continue to learn from her.

I also wish to thank a number of colleagues who contributed invaluable information and ideas to this project: Elizabeth Souritz, who kindly clarified many points raised in Lopukhov's texts; Selma Odom and Mary Trofimov, both of whom offered valuable historical data on Emile Jaques-Dalcroze; Stanley Rabinowitz, who generously shared with me ideas and research material on Akim Volynsky; Roland John Wiley, who offered advice on music rehearsal practices in nineteenth-century ballet; Giannandrea Poesio, who helped me enthusiastically with a number of points regarding steps and mime in the nineteenth-century classics; Marian Smith, who spent hours with me debating musical practices in nineteenth-century ballet and directing me toward important background material; Ann Hutchinson Guest, who gave up her time to decipher Stepanov notation for me and opened her library of Labanotation scores in order for me to make textual comparisons; Ivor Guest, for generously lending me his personal copies of Lopukhov's books; and Jennifer Thorp, who graciously enlightened me about structural principles in dance forms prior to the nineteenth-century and directed me to the relevant scholarly texts. I am deeply indebted to Galina Dobrovolskaya for her seminal work on Lopukhov, an inspiring source for my own research, and I acknowledge the Lopukhov Foundation for its important work in keeping the choreographer's legacy in public view.

I am grateful to a number of organizations for their help with this project, to the staff at the libraries that have supported my research, and especially to the staff at the New York Public

Library, for supplying me with a copy of Lopukhov's *Ballet Master and His Art;* to the Houghton Library of Harvard University (and specifically to Annette Fern, research and reference librarian) for supplying on microfilm several Stepanov scores of the nineteenth-century classics; to the Society of Dance History Scholars and the University of Surrey Roehampton, London, for sponsoring the translation of Russian material.

To my exemplary Studies editor, Lynn Garafola, I owe an enormous debt of gratitude. Ever since that initial march down Broadway when she urged me to submit a proposal for this project, she has supported me with ideas as to my own contribution, offered her own expert knowledge of the historical period, checked details in Russian sources, and helped with meticulous editing as well as preparation of the final manuscript. Without her commitment and enthusiasm, the final stages of the book would have been seen through neither so carefully nor so rapidly.

Special thanks, too, to Larraine Nicholas, my assistant in preparing the manuscript for presentation for press. The precision of her work, coupled with her own knowledge and attention to detail as a fine dance historian in her own right, helped me greatly in the most stressful period of the project.

Finally, my thanks to Howard Friend, my husband, who, as always, acted as first reader and offered the kind of criticism that gave me confidence when I needed it most.

WRITINGS ON BALLET AND MUSIC

Fedor Lopukhov, mid-1930s (From the Lincoln Kirstein Collection; Jerome Robbins Dance Division; The New York Public Library for the Performing Arts; Astor Lenox and Tildon Foundations)

This first publication in English of theoretical writings by the Russian choreographer Fedor Lopukhov (1886–1973) recognizes his seminal importance in the development of dance as an autonomous, nonnarrative art form during the twentieth century. It also indicates his role in theorizing a kind of dance that uses the model of music and reveals or visualizes musical structure. Both these approaches, nonnarrative and musically based, are key to twentieth-century dance. Lopukhov's 1925 treatise *The Ballet Master and His Art* (Puti baletmeistera), a substantial part of which has been translated here, is an important early expression of such theories of dance and music. Occasionally cited in English-language sources, it has long cried out for translation.[1]

Lopukhov's thinking about autonomous, nonnarrative dance is clearly in line with key modernist trends of the early twentieth century—above all, the rapid movement toward abstraction and emphasis on the properties particular to a given art medium. The ideal form that he introduces in the treatise is that of the "dance symphony," the stage realization of which has probably been the main reason for our knowing of the existence of the treatise at all. Lopukhov's *Dance Symphony: The Magnificence of the Universe* is a landmark in the history of ballet modernism. Set to Beethoven's Fourth Symphony, this ballet, which premiered in Petrograd (as St. Petersburg was renamed at the outset of the First World War),[2] is viewed today as seminal to the development of twentieth-century works that were modernist, music based, and grounded in the classical vocabulary. *Dance Symphony* was an important influence on the young George Balanchine, who danced in the premiere with members of his company, the Young Ballet, only a year before emigrating to the West in 1924.

Dance Symphony was given two performances, a private demonstration in 1922 in a rehearsal hall, followed by the public premiere at a benefit performance at the Petrograd Opera and Ballet Theater in 1923. Bringing a long evening to a late close, the work was poorly received by the first-night audience and critics. Indeed, with its mystical, grandiose section titles and lengthy program notes, it excited little more than irritation.[3] Lopukhov's treatise or book is thus important in explaining the theoretical principles behind *Dance Symphony*—a chapter is devoted to this topic alone—as well as the more general idea of symphonism in dance.

The Ballet Master and His Art also demonstrates that, like a number of other twentieth-century choreographers, including Balanchine, Lopukhov saw music as the force of liberation that would enable the development of a new, nonnarrative style of choreography. Music was both a model for theories of choreographic structure, small-scale as well as large, and a sophisticated complement to or stimulus for complex "symphonic" choreographies. Lopukhov's ideal relationship for music and dance, emphasized throughout the book, is one of synthesis, a true integration between the components of each medium.

The chapters selected for translation are those that illustrate Lopukhov's thinking about choreographic structure and its relations with music. They form a coherent unit in themselves and are supplemented by two essays—"The Choreography of the Shades Scene in *La Bayadère*" and "Petipa as Creator of the Choreographic Sonata Form"—both published in 1972 in *Choreographic Revelations* (Khoreograficheskie otkrovennosti) shortly before Lopukhov's death.[4] These two essays demonstrate Lopukhov's continuing interest in the theory of choreographic structure. Together with the excerpts from *The Ballet Master and His Art*, they offer a fascinating account of late-nineteenth-century ballet. An analysis of Lopukhov's account, with emphasis on musical considerations, is another focus of the present volume. The late nineteenth century witnessed the premiere of most of the ballets today regarded as classics, including *The Sleeping Beauty* (1890), *The Nutcracker* (1892), and *Swan Lake* (1894–1895). Lopukhov documents the repertory as he saw it in the early years of the twentieth century; he also provides a detailed musical-choreographic analysis of selected dances.

BIOGRAPHICAL AND POLITICAL BACKGROUND

Lopukhov tells us that he began work on *The Ballet Master and His Art* in 1916, the year his first substantial works, *The Dream* and *The Mexican Saloon,* were danced by members of the Maryinsky troupe at the Theater of Musical Drama in Petrograd.[5] With a score by Nikolai Shcherbachev, *The Dream* explored the correspondences between dance and musical structure advocated in the treatise. Lopukhov writes that he tried to harmonize his choreography with the orchestration, structuring of musical themes, counterpoint, and harmony.[6] It was natural for Lopukhov to use dancers from the Maryinsky Theater: he was himself a member of the company, which he joined in 1905 after graduating from its affiliated school, except for brief periods spent with the Bolshoi Ballet (1909–1910) and on tour with Anna Pavlova's company (1910–1911), when he paid his only visit to the United States.[7]

The 1917 Revolution and the ensuing civil war brought conditions of extreme hardship to the once privileged companies of the former Imperial Theaters. The Maryinsky Theater (now renamed the Petrograd Opera and Ballet Theater) continued to function, although there was little fuel and almost nothing for the dancers to eat. Conditions eased in 1921 with the advent of the New Economic Policy (NEP), which restored certain types of capitalism in order to stimulate the economy. But, even during the harsh times that followed the Revolution, theaters were packed, and studios of every kind were opening; the country was in the throes of theatrical and choreographic experiment. In the building of the new communist society, the arts were considered extremely important.

Nevertheless, opinion was divided over what should become

of the former Imperial Theaters. Lenin, for one, considered opera and ballet "landlord culture"[8] and pressed to have them closed down. But, thanks to the farsightedness of his Commissar of Enlightenment, Anatoly Lunacharsky, they survived as national showcases. In the concluding chapter of *The Ballet Master and His Art*, clearly written after the Revolution, Lopukhov takes a firm stand against those who criticize classical ballet as "useless," declaring it both classless and international in potential, and thus well suited to the new political régime.

In 1922, Lopukhov was appointed the artistic director of the former Maryinsky ballet. He was soon at work on *Dance Symphony*. At the same time, he devoted most of his energy to restoring the legacy of Marius Petipa, who had ruled the company for decades (he retired in 1904) and choreographed most of its repertory. In 1922, Lopukhov mounted the first postrevolutionary production of *The Sleeping Beauty;* this was followed by revivals of *Raymonda, Swan Lake,* and *Don Quixote.* He also produced a regular series of ballets of his own, including the first Soviet stagings of Stravinsky's *Firebird* (1921), *Pulcinella* (1926), and *Renard* (1927), ballets that Diaghilev's Ballets Russes had initially brought to the stage in the West. Not only did his ballets explore a range of themes, styles, and genres, but they also revealed his continuing interest in modernism and sophisticated dance structures. *Dance Symphony* is unusual in its degree of abstraction. By the second half of the 1920s, this was not a line of experiment Lopukhov was free to pursue.

Possibly because of the changing political climate, *The Ballet Master and His Art* was published not in the Soviet Union but in Berlin, which had experienced a huge influx of Russians after the Revolution. Petropolis, which brought it out, was an émigré house, which enjoyed greater editorial freedom than its Soviet counterparts but still had access to the Soviet market. Thus, it was able to publish a wide range of authors, including those writing inside the Soviet Union who found it difficult to publish their work at home.[9] Whether this was the case for Lopukhov is unclear.

Certainly, by the end of the 1920s, Lopukhov's formalist concerns were seen not only as being out-of-date but also politically suspect. As Stalin tightened his grip on the Soviet political apparatus in the years after Lenin's death in 1924, the relative freedom enjoyed by the arts since the Revolution was gradually curtailed. In 1934, at the First All-Union Congress of Soviet Writers, formal experiment (or "formalism," as it was referred to disparagingly) was eliminated entirely: henceforth, "socialist realism"—defined as being "national in form and socialist in content"—was to be the only acceptable form of Soviet art. Thus, the pluralism of Soviet dance in the 1920s gave way to a form of dramatic narrative, ballets that used plot and other traditional forms of representation as their primary content rather than dance vocabulary and structure. Vasily Tikhomirov's 1927 ballet for the Bolshoi, *The Red Poppy,* a revolutionary melodrama set in China, became the model for the new Soviet ballet.

Lopukhov did not immediately see the handwriting on the wall. In 1931 he choreographed *Bolt,* a satirical ballet on the subject of industrial espionage, to a score by Dmitri Shostakovich. The work was deemed a failure, and Lopukhov was asked to resign as director of the company, soon to be renamed the Kirov Ballet, although he returned to the position in 1944–1946 and again in 1951–1956.[10] Barred now from the company that had nurtured him, he formed a troupe at Leningrad's Maly Opera House, which he turned into a kind of laboratory for experiments in comic ballet. In 1935, he staged his second Shostakovich ballet, *The Bright Stream,* which was set on a collective farm and was heavily criticized for "formalism" and lack of understanding of rural peasant culture. Once again, Lopukhov was forced to resign as director. The following year, the ballet was remounted at the Bolshoi Theater. However, it quickly vanished when, in the same year, *Pravda* denounced the composer's controversial opera *Lady Macbeth of Mtsensk* (1934) in a severe Stalinist exercise in cultural control.[11]

By now, Lopukhov had largely completed his career as a working choreographer, although he was later to become an honored senior figure of the Russian ballet world. Instead, he concentrated on teaching and on supporting young choreographers. (Among his best-known protégés was Yuri Grigorovich, the longtime artistic director of the Bolshoi Ballet.) He directed the choreography department of the Leningrad Choreographic Institute from 1936 to 1941 and that of the Leningrad Conservatory from 1962 to 1973. Lopukhov was also a prolific writer, the author of numerous journal articles and, in addition to *The Ballet Master and His Art,* of two books that have informed this essay: the biographical *Sixty Years in Ballet,* published in 1966, and *Choreographic Revelations,* his 1972 primer on choreography and performance.

ARTISTIC BACKGROUND

The Revolution of 1917 was a watershed for the arts, promoting certain types of art and instituting new organizational structures for its production. "October catalyzed and mobilized a need for the new," the historian Sally Banes has written; "it also sparked debate about the value of the old."[12] Symbolism, which saw art as visionary, a quest for essence rather than literal representation, became a force in Russia in the 1890s, first in literature, then in the visual arts with the founding of the journal *Mir iskusstva* (World of Art), edited by Serge Diaghilev, the future director of the Ballets Russes. A high point came in 1906 with Alexander Blok's *Fairground Booth,* brought to the stage by Vsevolod Meyerhold. By 1910, however, other "isms" had displaced symbolism as a catalyst for experiment. Among the most important was futurism, which attracted poets like Vladimir Mayakovsky, Alexei Kruchenikh, and Velimir Khlebnikov, all of whom were actively involved in the avant-garde theater. Mayakovsky was the author of *Mystery-Bouffe* (1918); Kruchenikh wrote the libretto and Khlebnikov the prologue of the 1913 futurist opera *Victory over the Sun.*

Futurism, in Russia often in tandem with cubism as cubo-futurism, also permeated the visual arts. Among the leaders of this movement were Natalia Goncharova and Mikhail Larionov. In 1910, they formed the Knave of Diamonds exhibition group (the name was chosen because of its lack of symbolist associations) and in 1912 the Donkey's Tail group, which advocated the brilliant color and neoprimitivist folk forms made famous in their many collaborations with the Ballets Russes. Kazimir Malevich, who exhibited with the Donkey's Tail and designed the sets and costumes for *Victory over the Sun*, made the passage to pure abstraction on the eve of the First World War, with "suprematist" paintings like *Black Square*, which depicted a geometric form against a white background. This was the artistic Left that on the eve of the 1917 Revolution pushed Russia to the forefront of the avant-garde.

By Lopukhov's own account, he first became interested in contemporary developments in art, music, and literature around 1910. He was especially drawn to the art of the Left and to the poetry of Alexander Blok, although his interests spanned the many "isms" that dotted the era's artistic landscape.[13] This continued after the Revolution, as well. He admired the constructivists, artists who had placed the advanced forms of modernism at the service of the new Soviet state, and imagined great architectural designs, like Vladimir Tatlin's rotating *Monument to the Third International* (1919–1920) that were never to be built. Stage design was equally reconceived; for Meyerhold's production of *The Magnanimous Cuckold* (1922), Lubov Popova designed a totally functional set, a multilevel construction with platforms, flywheels, and a staircase that acknowledged the triumph of the machine age.[14] The old theatrical verities had gone.

However, even in the early post-Soviet years, not all art represented a quest for new forms. Generations of artists overlapped, with poets like Anna Akhmatova continuing to write along more traditional lines and painters like Isaak Brodsky pursuing a more realist or representational vein. Some artists, including Malevich and Wassily Kandinsky, despite their interest in exploring nonobjective forms, also harbored spiritual or mystical concerns akin to those of the symbolists. This, as we shall see, was the case with Lopukhov. Moreover, as a choreographer who believed in the need to preserve the classical inheritance (both the language of the danse d'école and the repertory

of works built up by preceding generations of choreographers),
Lopukhov was indirectly aligned with artists, writers, and others
interested in more classical forms of expression. As head of
the former Maryinsky ballet company, his supporters included
Alexandre Benois, who had designed a number of ballets for the
Ballets Russes, including *Petrouchka* (1911), as well as plays for
the Moscow Art Theater; Alexander Golovin, a designer who
had worked closely with Meyerhold during his career as a director at the Imperial Theaters; Boris Asafiev, a composer, musicologist, and critic (who also wrote under the pseudonym Igor
Glebov); and the conductor Emile Cooper.[15] All were now
members of the theater administration. Asafiev, as we shall see,
was especially important as a musical adviser to Lopukhov, his
long association with the Maryinsky beginning with his appoint-
ment in 1910 as a ballet pianist, after which he created twenty-
eight ballet scores.

In *The Ballet Master and His Art*, Lopukhov reveals little
sympathy for dance forms other than classical ballet. Most of
these new forms had their center in Moscow, where a number
of experimental studios opened in the aftermath of the Revolution. The new Russian capital was also the home of Kasian
Goleizovsky's Chamber Ballet and Nikolai Foregger's workshop
MASTFOR.[16] Isadora Duncan, whose visits to Russia began in
1904, set up her own school in Moscow in 1921, and a Choreological Laboratory was established in the Russian Academy
of Artistic Sciences (RAKhN) in 1923.[17] In postrevolutionary
Petrograd, dance activity centered chiefly on one institution,
the Opera and Ballet Theater, and remained largely in the
hands of one choreographer, Lopukhov himself.

Yet Lopukhov's work shows an active response to experiments in the other arts. According to the critic Alexei Gvozdev,
Lopukhov's production of *Pulcinella*, which he staged in 1926,
revealed the influence of Meyerhold's antiliterary experiments,
as well as something of Evgeny Vakhtangov's "fantastic realism" and Alexander Tairov's "synthetic" or total theater.[18] He
was interested in contemporary treatments of folklore, especially the buffoon play, which he used as a model in staging

Night on Bald Mountain (1924) and *Renard*. He followed the productions of Sergei Radlov's Theater of Popular Comedy, during its brief existence from 1920 to 1922, and the ethnographic work of the Experimental Theater, headed by Vsevolod Vsevolodsky-Gerngross.[19] Lopukhov introduced Soviet themes into his 1924 production *The Red Whirlwind,* a dance allegory that was the first ballet specifically about the October Revolution. In *Bolt* there were stage formations and multibodied pyramid configurations representing the Soviet symbol of the star: "We saw before us the discoveries of the Blue Blouse and TRAM [groups] and dreamed of doing something of equal value.... We were attracted to the possibility of putting into dance the motifs of political satire."[20] However, as Elizabeth Souritz has pointed out, by 1931 satire and agitprop were out of step with the conservative spirit of the times.

Like other, more progressive choreographers in the 1920s, including Foregger and Goleizovsky, Lopukhov was influenced by the constructivist movement. His dances used machinelike movement in mass formations and employed the stage space in new ways, with the choreography unfolding on and around mobile platforms and screens. He commissioned the constructivist sets of *Pulcinella* and *The Nutcracker* (1929) from Vladimir Dmitriev (a pupil of Meyerhold who collaborated with Balanchine in the direction of the Young Ballet and became a leading Soviet theater designer) and those of *Bolt* from Tatiana Bruni and Georgii Korshikov.[21] Lopukhov was a latecomer to constructivism, and his involvement with it continued until relatively late. Indeed, by the end of the 1920s, this movement, whose goal had been to reach a mass proletarian audience, had been branded as formalist and politically suspect. Like other avant-garde artistic movements, it had to bow before the political triumph of socialist realism.

Lopukhov also embraced the work of modernist composers in the 1920s. He used the music of Stravinsky and Shostakovich, and that of Vladimir Deshevov in *The Red Whirlwind*. Deshevov was a leading avant-gardist associated with TRAM, and his "constructivist" music for the "industrial melodrama"

Rails (1926) inspired Darius Milhaud to pronounce him a "genius, original to the highest degree."[22] On the other hand, Lopukhov also turned to Rheinhold Glière (for *The Red Poppy*), a composer who set the standard for the antimodernist ballet music that flourished under socialist realism. Another such composer was Boris Asafiev, whose arrangement of music by Grieg Lopukhov was to use in *The Ice Maiden* (1927). Asafiev had already selected the music for an earlier ballet on the same theme, Pavel Petrov's *Solveig* (1922).[23] Lopukhov's version turned out to be one of his most successful ballets.

On the whole, the scores that Lopukhov used illustrate the major shift in the style of music used for ballet that took place during the early decades of the twentieth century. Promoted by the theories and practices of such artists as Fokine and Isadora Duncan, the short numbers—alternating pantomime and dances—typical of nineteenth-century ballet gave way to more symphonic, through-composed musical constructions, either specially composed or borrowed from the concert hall. Even if Lopukhov's *Dance Symphony* was atypical of his work at large, the symphonic nature of the score was in keeping with contemporary trends in ballet music.

Lopukhov's ideal compositional method required a certain understanding of musical technicalities. There are references to his playing the guitar and piano, attending orchestra rehearsals, and studying score reading for a year with the conductor Emile Cooper as preparation for his work on *Dance Symphony*.[24] In *The Ballet Master and His Art,* he states that, to attain the true integration of music and dance, it is essential for the choreographer to examine the details of musical timbre and texture contained in the full score, as opposed to the piano or two-violin répétiteur traditionally used in rehearsal (see p. 57). Yet Lopukhov limited himself to what was important to him for choreographic purposes. The musical discussion in his writings is generally competent without revealing sophisticated analytical skills. One or two of his observations would be surprising from an educated musician, or perhaps they are a sign of sloppy thinking. Lopukhov claims, for instance, that the two-violin répétiteur preceded the orchestral score. The other way round makes greater musical sense: a composer would be most likely to conceive of musical harmony incorporating the full bass range prior to creating any "reduction" into the high register of two violins (see p. 57).[25] Lopukhov also uses a misleading time signature in his essay "Petipa as Creator of the Choreographic Sonata Form": the musical example suggests $\frac{3}{4}$, not $\frac{6}{8}$ (see p. 163 and music example 1):

Music example 1

THE THEORETICAL WRITINGS:
IDEAS AND INFLUENCES

Responding to details of timbre and texture in the full musical score is an example of the synthesis, the harmony between music and dance, that is an explicit ideal of *The Ballet Master and His Art*. In this respect, Lopukhov was drawing on a widely held early twentieth-century theory of equivalence between one art medium and another and a belief in the possibility of translation between media. At the root of these ideas was the romantic idea of organicism, wholeness, a longstanding tradition in the arts of transcending dualities. A more immediate source was the symbolist aesthetic: the mystical platonism based on the notion that all the arts originated from a single divine truth, as different refractions of the same celestial beam. Other sources were the theory of correspondences stemming from poetry, especially that of Baudelaire, and the idea of *Gesamtkunstwerk*—the fusion of the arts—associated with the music dramas of Richard Wagner.[26]

In Russia, synesthesia emerged as an artistic concern in the 1890s. The idea was vigorously promoted by Diaghilev, and, with his manifestation of the *Gesamtkunstwerk* in ballet, it remained important well into the 1920s. Alexander Scriabin, the most highly regarded of all Russian composers until his work fell into disfavor in the mid-1920s, subscribed to the notion of a multisensual mystical art, blending sound, color, smell, touch, music, poetry, and gesture. His *Prometheus, Poem of Fire* (1910) introduced a color keyboard, the aim being to envelop the listener in color and light. Likewise, Kandinsky experimented with synesthesia while living as a young artist in Munich in the 1910s, and this preoccupation continued into his maturity: his primary concern was with the mutual exchanges between visual and auditory elements. A founder of the Choreological Laboratory in Moscow, he remained in close touch with the organization even after settling in Germany in 1921, where he encouraged synthetic experiments involving a number of art forms. *Zangesi,* a theater piece presented by an amateur company of the Experimental Theater of the Museum of Artistic Culture in Petrograd the same year that *Dance Symphony* was premiered, stemmed from a different basis. The work was based on a poem by Khlebnikov (the event was dedicated to his memory), a construction in which the sounds of words were of primary importance rather than their meaning. The constructivist designer Vladimir Tatlin fashioned his set according to a theory of correspondences among colors, forms, and sounds.[27]

For artists of the period, regardless of discipline, music was seen as offering a model for spiritual, poetic experience; apparently the most abstract of the arts, it evoked the true essence of reality. For dance, there was the belief that music could be a liberating force, the starting point for dance inspiration. Dance was also thought to share an equivalence or deep relationship with music that stemmed from what was thought to be the gestural basis of all the arts.[28] In Russia, especially, much avant-garde dance was inspired by the imported traditions of Duncan and the Swiss music pedagogue Emile Jaques-Dalcroze, with their concomitant aesthetics of music interpretation or visualization. Duncan, aiming to express the *Geist,* or spirit of the music, or the feelings it suggested to her, turned to the great composers of the past, both for inspiration and in order to be in harmony, a state of wholeness, with history.[29] Dalcroze, by contrast, developed a method known as eurhythmics, a physical as well as musical form of training aimed at heightening the rhythmic sensitivity in musicians. Introduced to Russia around 1909, the method was vigorously promoted by Prince Sergei Volkonsky, the former director of the Imperial Theaters, and its influence spread beyond dance into the fields of cinema and theater.[30] Dalcroze's approach was to develop a list of structural rather than emotional equivalents, what he called common elements, between music and "moving plastic."

In 1923, the Choreological Laboratory in Moscow created a Studio of Synthetic Dance. The studio was directed by Inna Chernetskaia, who acknowledged its debt to the symbolist idea of artistic synesthesia: "I think that the path of the free dance of the future will occur in an organic fusion of the three arts of painting, music, and dance."[31] We must not forget, too, the precedent for Lopukhov's *Dance Symphony* of Gorsky's setting of Alexander Glazunov's Fifth Symphony at the Bolshoi Theater in 1916. However, the Gorsky ballet does not seem to have been an exposition of carefully theorized relationships between music and dance or a specific negotiation with musical form. Lopukhov never saw the work; indeed, he tells us that he only heard about it much later, having spent the years 1914–1916 in military service with only intermittent visits to Petrograd.[32]

In *The Ballet Master and His Art,* Lopukhov outlines four stages in the developing relationship between music and dance: dance "with music," dance "to the accompaniment of music," dance "set to music," and, finally, the ideal of true integration of the two media, dance "in the image of music." Dance "with music" refers to the style in which virtually no correspondence exists between the two media. Lopukhov gives examples from the Petipa repertory of basic metrical differentiation, for instance, two-beat dance units set against triple meter in the music (producing a contrapuntal effect). This practice Lopukhov regards as a holdover from an earlier time when lack of correspondence was the norm. In the case of dance "to the accompaniment of music," the music plays a secondary role, which is what happens with the music of specialist ballet composers like Cesare Pugni and Ludwig Minkus. Here, Petipa's approach is to adhere to the repeating metrical structure within the musical phrase, without attention to other changing musical details of rhythm pattern or melodic curve. Lopukhov is again critical of the lack of harmony that arises between music and dance, but he perceives even less harmony when dance is "set to music," for instance, in the ballets of Tchaikovsky, where music plays the dominant role. Integration, or in Lopukhov's phrase, dance "in the image of music," means true harmony between the media. The implication here is that music and dance have also reached a stage of internal complexity, an ideal "symphonic" form, according to their respective terms.

The following are examples from Lopukhov's list of fundamental rules on integrating dance and music (see pp. 146–147):

- Choreographic and musical themes must work together, not cut across each other. For example, a musical theme that suggests upward flight cannot be combined with a choreographic theme that suggests crawling, even if the two themes are identical in terms of rhythm.
- There must be a unity of the musical and choreographic forms.
- Emotional climaxes in the dance must coincide with emotional climaxes in the music.
- The curve of the dance must correspond to the curve of the music.
- The color of the dance movements must match the color of the orchestration.
- Major keys must be equated with en dehors and minor with en dedans.
- Key changes must be reproduced choreographically.

Yet Lopukhov does not advocate a totally rigid formula for choreographing music. Sometimes, he admits, decisions have to be made to follow one (the most important) aspect of musical structure while ignoring another (see p. 144). As he writes:

"When the musical line speaks of upward flight, concern as to whether the dance movements fit the measure of the music must not be allowed to override other considerations to the extent that a contradiction arises between music and dance."

Lopukhov mentions both Duncan and Dalcroze in his early writings and is dismissive of them both. In a 1922 article that is referred to in *The Ballet Master and His Art* (see p. 72), he criticizes Duncan's choice of subject matter for Tchaikovsky's Sixth Symphony, the *Pathétique* (1916), as an insulting imposition that bears no resemblance to the intentions of the composer.[33] Duncan responded to the music as a young, carefree woman, then as a leader rousing the crowd to challenge and battle, and finally as a grieving earth mother.[34] At the same time, Lopukhov denigrates as mechanistic Dalcroze's proposals for relationships between music and dance (see p. 137): "In striving to integrate dance and music we may mechanize dance by reproducing only the duration and tempo of the notes in the musical score. This was what happened in the case of the system developed by Emile Jaques-Dalcroze. In my opinion stage productions based upon his system are a total failure; I have never seen anything in the work of the followers of Dalcroze other than the use of arms and legs for the purpose of 'reproducing notes.'" Lopukhov claims that the ballet choreographer has a far richer palette of movement from which to choose: "choreography offers countless possibilities for achieving complete union between dance and music, none of which will lead to the pitfall of gymnastics" (see p. 142).

Primarily, as Lopukhov suggests, Dalcroze developed techniques for visualizing beat, meter, and details of rhythmic pattern. Nevertheless, his work did encourage a response to other musical parameters. The following list demonstrates a range of structural equivalents between music and the body in movement, or "moving plastic," as he called it:

Pitch	Position and direction of gestures in space
Intensity of sound	Muscular dynamics

Timbre	Diversity in corporal forms (the sexes)
Duration	Duration
Time	Time
Rhythm	Rhythm
Rests	Pauses
Melody	Continuous succession of isolated movements
Counterpoint	Opposition of movements
Chords	Arresting of associated gestures (or gestures in groups)
Harmonic successions	Succession of associated movements (or of gestures in groups)
Phrasing	Phrasing
Construction (form)	Distribution of movements in space and time
Orchestration (*vide* timbre)	Opposition and combination of diverse corporal forms (the sexes)[35]

In the Dalcroze method of training, there were also exercises in counterpoint: within the body, for instance, arms beating different rhythms from the feet or between movement and music.[36]

There is a striking similarity between the theories and practices of Dalcroze and those of Lopukhov, however much the choreographer disparaged Dalcroze's thought. For both, each musical parameter has a movement equivalent. Examples of what might be called "rhythmic gymnastics" can be perceived in Lopukhov's work; for example, the counterpoint within the body in the Infernal Dance of *Firebird*—where "the legs of the dancers did the pas de basque to a two-beat measure while the arms moved to three beats"—and in the adagio movement of *Dance Symphony,* when Alexandra Danilova, who danced in the original cast, moved "her legs to a two-count phrase and her arms to a three-count phrase."[37] Lopukhov's movement vocabulary was generally quite different from the "natural" barefoot vocabulary of Dalcroze, but there is no denying that a close relationship between movement and musical structures forms a link across their respective styles.

Fokine was the choreographer whose musicality Lopukhov admired above all others when he penned his treatise. He applauds his mature practice of attending to the orchestral score, rather than a reduced arrangement of it (see p. 67), and praises him for possessing "a high degree of musical sensitivity" and for improving on Petipa's practice. *Chopiniana* (1908), which Fokine restaged for the Ballets Russes as *Les Sylphides* (1909), demonstrates a clear affinity with Lopukhov's own approach to music. In a 1923–1924 interview with the British music critic Edwin Evans, Fokine described the relationship of soloists to melody and corps to accompaniment in the second half of the opening Nocturne, op. 32, no. 2: "[The corps] mark the rhythmic beat whilst the principals are drawing their line of dance to the melody and harmonizing its rise and fall with the rise and fall of their movements." He went on to analyze the whole of the solo Waltz, op. 70, no. 1, as a visualization of musical structure:

I set my soloist four tasks. Firstly she has to mark the rhythmic beat of a valse. This means that in roughly every other bar she dances either some valse step or steps with three changes of weight; or else marks the three beats by gradually lowering her hand (in the third phrase); or beats one foot on the other (at the end of the fourth phrase). This marking of the beat (or pulse) otherwise than by the feet is a particular feature of some Russian folk dances which I utilized in order to make my classical dance seem more rhythmically sensitive.

Secondly, the dancer's movements follow the pattern of the melody. As the music soars up and down in an arpeggio and is then held on a high note during the first phrase, so the soloist soars upwards in a *grand jeté en avant*, momentarily holds herself in the air, falls into a valse step, then, as the note is held, poses in an *arabesque*. Something similar happens in the second phrase where, instead of marking the beat with a valse step, she springs three times, each time lowering the leg very slightly to match the descending notes to which these *jetés* are danced. In the third phrase, the soloist not only marks the beats but also the descending notes with the lowering of her hand. During the fifth phrase she swings up and down with the lilt of the melody, turns in *attitude* as a high note is held, then she "embroiders" round her high note by making a circle round that same spot *sur les pointes* before crossing the stage to the opposite side with a long held *arabesque*.

Thirdly I allow the formal musical structure to dictate the choregraphic [*sic*] pattern. The first musical phrase of sixteen bars is repeated, so the second four short dance phrases are also a repeat of the first four movements. But because Glazunov made some slight changes in his orchestration of the repeat, I make slight changes in my choreography [*sic*]. For example, the *grand jeté en avant* of the first passage becomes a *grand jeté entrelacé*. The third, and first eight bars of the fourth musical phrase state new ideas, so does the dancer, but the last eight bars of the latter restate the third phrase and the dancer similarly repeats her long *arabesque*. But instead of dropping her front hand gradually to the descending notes, she presses both hands softly outwards, as if she were calling her fellow sylphs to the dance. The final phrase is a repeat of the last two bars during which the dancer turns and disappears from sight. This slight variation in the last two bars of a phrase I have noted throughout. The valse is made up of short four-bar phrases merging into each other, with an imperfect cadence at the end of each sixteen bars. The dancer is guided by these links in the musical continuity and usually repeats her *enchaînements* three times, but the fourth time she does not make a perfect repeat because she has to draw her line into a preparation for the next phrase and in the last *enchaînement* prepare the way for the next dancer.

Fourthly, I allow the musical structure to determine the floor pattern so that the circling of a valse is continually being made visible as the dancer circles the stage, or turns in her *grands jetés entrelacés, pirouettes* and other steps.[38]

The likeness here to Lopukhov's theory of music is striking. Furthermore, like Lopukhov, Fokine took from the music what served his choreographic purposes, thus acknowledging the need for choreographic freedom. One major distinction between musical and dance structures in *Les Sylphides* is their different use of repetition, less in the dance than in the music. New step combinations appear to repeating music, offering alternative responses to musical detail.

Through Fokine, Lopukhov was persuaded of the possibilities of nonnarrative choreography and dance "symphonism." In *Sixty Years in Ballet,* he wrote that it was Fokine's 1913 ballet *Les Préludes,* with its generalized theme of man's struggle between life and death, that first inspired him.[39] He also singled out Fokine's dances in the opera *Orphée* (1911), *The Polovtsian Dances* (1909), and (unsurprisingly) *Chopiniana* as demonstrating symphonism.

Lopukhov's "symphonic" principles are concerned with unity, organicism, and thematic development, or the interweaving and variation of dance material. These concepts were borrowed from any number of musical models. But notions of "symphony" and "symphonism" had special resonance within the Russian context of the time. While the musical symphony was read as a mirror for life, the idea of a "symphonic society," the organic, united revolutionary society within which the individual would find fulfillment was also important.[40]

"Symphonism" was a commonly stated ideal for both dance and dance music construction during the early Soviet period. Witness Asafiev's comments about the manner in which *The Sleeping Beauty* score supported dance, not only as "defined dance formulas" (implying the subordination of all musical elements to meter) but as "dance formulas complicated and deepened by the transformation process of symphonic development."[41] Asafiev's idea of transformative thematic processes resonates with Lopukhov's own notions of construction: notions of "symphonic" form, "choreographic themes that conflict, contract, and develop in parallel with each other," as opposed to the "random selection of dance movements" (see p. 98).

Though Lopukhov's "symphonism" encompasses small- as well as large-scale works, the latter clearly have the greatest potential for sophisticated treatment, with small units or sections nesting within larger ones and because of the possibility of thematic referencing over a long time span. He finds isolated examples in the work of Petipa and Lev Ivanov, just as in the ballet scores of Tchaikovsky and Glazunov. Two-thirds of the second act of *Giselle* he considers to be conceived symphonically. Here, he writes, four motifs are elaborated: port de bras, arabesque, saut de basque, and jeté (see p. 98). Another, more significant example, according to Lopukhov, is the last act of *Swan Lake,* before Rothbart's entrance: here the port de bras motif of the grieving swans is developed through a variety of positions by the whole ensemble (see p. 100). Toward the end of his life, Lopukhov described the grand pas in *Paquita* as a "classical symphony of dance" (see "Petipa as Creator of the Choreographic Sonata Form," p. 166) and noted approvingly the "symphonic" principles that underlay Grigorovich's first major ballet, *The Stone Flower* (1957).[42]

Lopukhov was clearly inspired by musical concepts and categories, which he applied directly to dance. Thus, in *Choreographic Revelations,* he refers to "dance tonality" and to variations of dance material as being "in different keys" (see p. 175). He applies the metaphor of sonata form to the Shades scene in *La Bayadère* and to the pas de six in *The Daughter of Pharaoh.* In neither case is the music in sonata form (that is, with exposition, development, and recapitulation), and Lopukhov adopts a free notion of the form for the choreography. First, there is an exposition or opening section, then a development or elaboration, and finally a reprise, dénouement, or finale/coda. But the latter remains developmental, certainly in *La Bayadère;* it is not the same as musical recapitulation, which, broadly speaking, provides a symmetry with the exposition, while confirming the tonic or home key after deviating from it. Nonetheless, the analogy with this hallowed and sophisticated musical form suggests something of Lopukhov's ambition to place choreographic structural values on a par with those of music.

If music constituted Lopukhov's model for abstraction and structural principles that could be borrowed for dance, a body of dance theory focusing on movement- and choreography-based issues also arose in this period. It, too, supported Lopukhov's approach.[43] André Levinson and Akim Volynsky, two Russian critics of symbolist and later neoclassical persuasion, analyzed movement in terms of spatial patterns, the dynamics and structure of phrases, the linearity and turnout fundamental to classical style.[44] Theirs was a kind of "exalted idealism,"[45] with its basis in the formulae of ballet but combined with a meticulous analytical approach to movement and its structures and a belief in the autonomy of the medium. In a similar spirit, Bronislava Nijinska began her 1919 choreographic treatise with the words "Movement is the principal element of dancing."[46] Thus, she diminished the centrality of the libretto in the ballets of Fokine and other Diaghilev choreographers.

Lopukhov mentions Volynsky approvingly in *The Ballet Master and His Art*, singling him out for his understanding of classical dance and sharing his belief that individual movements harbored particular meanings (see p. 150). Thus, the unfolding of the leg after a grand plié in the Adagio movement of *Dance Symphony* is seen as a plant-like activity (see p. 93), and en dedans/croisé and en dehors/effacé alignments are read as messages of containment or expansion implying concomitant psychological states.[47] Lopukhov's view of Volynsky is that "he was the first to try to explain the meaning of each dance movement, which I, as a representative of choreography, welcome enthusiastically ... while disagreeing with the critic Volynsky in the details of explaining dance movements, I could not fail to welcome his explanation—the first such explanation—of the great essence of choreographic art."[48] Reading these words, no one would suspect the bad feeling that existed between Lopukhov and Volynsky after the Revolution, when the latter connived against Lopukhov in favor of having Nicolas Legat take over the directorship of the former Maryinsky company.

Levinson went unmentioned in Lopukhov's treatise. In all likelihood, the reason for this was that, at the time of its publication, the critic was in disgrace, not only because of his conservative views but also because he was an émigré, having left the Soviet Union in 1921. In *Sixty Years,* Lopukhov recognizes him as a thoughtful, serious critic, while admitting that he did not always agree with him.[49] Certainly, Levinson did not share Lopukhov's view of equivalence between movement and meaning or his theory of visualizing musical ideas and structures; he considered artistic synthesis a rudimentary stage of development and deplored the approach to music of Dalcroze, Duncan, and Fokine.[50]

Neither Levinson nor Volynsky advocated the use of purely symphonic music. Levinson thought that music should be "appended to the dance." "The aim of choreography," he asserted, "is not the interpretation of pure musical forms, but the formation of dance music from within the spirit of the dance itself."[51] Volynsky maintained that the combination of dance-based ("aural-flexional") and symphonic ("sonic-spiritual") styles was the best solution for ballet music: the "dansant" impetus remained essential.[52] Nevertheless, the theory of movement structures as a foundation for artistic idealism, for escape from the material world, is one of fundamental importance to them both, as well as to Lopukhov.

THE DANCE SYMPHONY:
FROM PROGRAM TO REALIZATION

Notions of idealism and connection with the nonmaterial world are evident in the program for *Dance Symphony* that appears in *The Ballet Master and His Art.* The theme is the glory of the cosmos, the organic relationship between earth and the heavens, and the triumph of life over death. The Joy of Existence, Lopukhov tells us, comes from the realization that the individual is an integral part of the cosmos: "The life of every being is a moment in eternity.... The sum of all lives is the universe" (see p. 94).

Lopukhov's cosmic vision had deep resonance for an artistic community riven by apocalyptic concerns, Promethean visions, and utopian dreams. The later symbolists saw art as having a theurgic purpose, imbued with cosmic significance and able to transform a world in urgent need of regeneration. Among those who shared this view were the writers Andrey Bely, Alexander Blok, and Vyacheslav Ivanov, all of whom were deeply influenced by the mystical philosopher Vladimir Solovyov, as well as by the composer Alexander Scriabin. Other artists developed theories of man as victor over nature in his conquest of space. Among them was Malevich, who enjoined his fellow men to "seize [the world] from the hands of nature and build a new world belonging to [man] himself."[53] "In man," he noted elsewhere, "in his consciousness lies the striving for space, the desire to break away from the planet Earth."[54] *Victory over the Sun,* the futurist opera designed by Malevich in 1913, depicted the strong men of the future capturing the sun. In the postrevolutionary era, propaganda often assumed a kind of religious zeal. The constructivists envisioned man as a supermachine, in ultimate control of all other machines, a demigod of the space-age industrial era.

Although initially Lopukhov preferred to have specially composed music for *Dance Symphony,* by 1921–1922 he had settled on Beethoven's Fourth Symphony.[55] Beethoven was an unsurprising choice of composer in this postrevolutionary period, though certain musicologists apparently claimed that Lopukhov's philosophy was "alien to the nature of … [the] Fourth Symphony."[56] Above all other composers at the time, Beethoven was revered as a revolutionary hero; indeed, he was seen as the composer most intimately associated with the French Revolution. Performances of his Ninth Symphony and his opera *Fidelio,* for instance, played an important part in the 1918 anniversary celebrations of the October Revolution.[57] Isadora Duncan had long promoted Beethoven's music as a stimulus for dance, staging such large-scale works as his *Moonlight* (ca. 1904) and *Pathétique* (1916) sonatas and his Seventh Symphony (1904).

The program issued for the premiere of *Dance Symphony* paraphrases and condenses material ultimately published in *The Ballet Master and His Art.* Lopukhov wrote the libretto with the help of his friend Vasily Gustavovich von Struve, the husband of his elder sister Evgenia Fedorovna Lopukhova.[58] The program was illustrated with silhouette drawings by Pavel Goncharov.[59] Here is how the ballet fitted Beethoven's score:

First Movement, Adagio: Introduction: The Birth of Light— The Birth of the Sun
Allegro Vivace: Life in Death and Death in Life
Second movement, Adagio: Thermal Energy
Third movement, Scherzo: The Joy of Existence
Fourth movement, Allegro ma non troppo: Perpetual Motion

As Lopukhov suggests (see p. 72), he felt free to reorder the titled sections of the work for the ballet. Life in Death and Death in Life, for instance, was not danced immediately prior to the Conclusion, as Lopukhov had originally intended, but much earlier, immediately after the First Movement Adagio.

In the First Movement Adagio, according to the dance historian Elizabeth Souritz, "eight youths crossed the proscenium in a chain. They covered their eyes with one hand and with the other seemed to grope their way through the gloom. Fixing their gaze upward, in the distance, eight women moved after them."[60] In the Allegro Vivace: Life in Death and Death in Life, themes of motion and immobility were intertwined. Following the Adagio Second Movement, which is discussed later, the Scherzo (The Joy of Existence) offered folk and grotesque movement elements: Lopukhov believed that such movement could be incorporated into dance symphonies alongside classical vocabulary. Perpetual Motion, which brought back the entire cast of eighteen and alluded to the triumphant codas of nineteenth-century ballets, ended with a Conclusion that included the famous spiral tableau captured in one of Goncharov's drawings. Symphonic ensembles were featured throughout the ballet, choreography for groups from which soloists emerged, a principle that Lopukhov developed with great sophistication in *The Ice Maiden.*

Working on *Dance Symphony* with the Beethoven score,

Lopukhov took the opportunity to illustrate his theory of musical-choreographic synthesis. The most important source for the ballet's dance text is Lopukhov's choreographic notebook. Here he transcribed the dances alongside their music, using diagrams and ballet terminology. His biographer Galina Dobrovolskaya has deciphered the opening Adagio crossing of the ballet in terms of step-for-note dancing, exact rhythmic duplication (see music example 2): "In the introduction to the Fourth Symphony ... the dancers took one step in the first bar, where the orchestra played one note, then two steps in each of the second and third bars, each of which contained two notes, four steps in the fourth bar, which consisted of four quarter-notes, one step in the fifth—one-note—bar, and so on."[61]

A videorecording of the Thermal Energy Adagio, as reconstructed in 1986 by Nikita Dolgushin for dancers of Leningrad Conservatory's Choreographic Institute, further illustrates the musical-choreographic principles articulated in *The Ballet Master and His Art.*[62] Citing Volynsky, Lopukhov had described the expressive content of this section: "In a newspaper article Akim Volynsky remarked that a full downward plié with the subsequent extension of the leg to one side made him think of natural growth stimulated by spring sunshine. This is exactly the impression that must be created by the Thermal Energy adagio. It must possess an insinuating quality and an internal balance. Nothing is static, not even for the briefest moment. In sum: the Thermal Energy adagio consists of slowly unfolding choreographic movements." In the reconstruction, a group of men perform posé coupé to the introductory accompaniment with its long-short rhythm and up-down pitch contour (see music example 3). When this pattern changes (bars 2–8), the men follow the new rising contour (the rhythm is the same as before) with a posé coupé followed by a step, temps levé, the sequence progressing forward and then backward. Meanwhile the women perform the legato melody line, in the manner referred to earlier, with a grand plié, sustained unfolding of the legs, arabesques, and ports de bras. In bar 9, when the initial accompaniment pattern is heard again in unison across the orchestral ensemble,

Symphony No. 4

I

Adagio ♩= 66

L. van Beethoven, Op. 60
1770 - 1827

B. & H. 8451   Printed in England

Music example 2

the solo women and men combine correspondingly in unison posés coupés. Clearly, Lopukhov worked very closely with musical detail. Later, Lopukhov responds to the lightening orchestral texture and focus on a solo clarinet, bars 28–31: the men stand still, and the two women move between them. In bars 55–59, a similar passage of thinner musical texture, the two women run in direct response to the two highlighted violin lines.

At bar 65, the recapitulation within the music's sonata form structure begins, shortened and modified in accordance with the requisite shift in tonal organization (to end in the home key). Lopukhov follows the thematic recapitulations in the music with corresponding recapitulations of the choreography.

Any reconstruction raises questions: how detailed were Lopukhov's choreographic notes, what were the problems in interpreting them, how reliable are the memories of surviving members of the original cast? Alexandra Danilova, who danced in the production, was present at the screening of the Dolgushin videorecording in New York in 1991 and corrected a passage "during which the 'Danilova' ballerina should have kept her back to the audience."[63] Even if other details might be corrected, the reconstruction supports totally the theories put forth in *The Ballet Master and His Art*.

In his later writings, Lopukhov continued to stand by *Dance Symphony*. However, he now emphasized the centrality of the musical and theoretical aspects of the work, while admitting that the conflict between the demands of the theme and those of the music was irresolvable. "The more successful I was in reproducing the musical ideas of Beethoven in movement," he wrote in *Sixty Years in Ballet*, "the further I departed from the theme of 'the magnificence of the universe' that had inspired me."[64] He also acknowledged that it would have been better to use the titles of the musical movements, rather than his own grandiose titles.[65] An alternative would have been specially composed music instead of the Beethoven. In short, Lopukhov now admitted that his main idea of having dance represent symphonic music got lost in this production.

Music example 3

Lopukhov's plans to choreograph other symphonies—Beethoven's Fifth Symphony, Tchaikovsky's Fourth Symphony, and Liszt's *Faust* Symphony—came to nothing. After the triumph of socialist realism, it was not until the "thaw" of the late 1950s and early 1960s that ballets set to symphonic music and without concrete dramatic content once again became acceptable, if only briefly.[66]

THE BALLET MASTER AND HIS ART AND THE LATE-NINETEENTH-CENTURY BALLET REPERTORY

Lopukhov's account of the late-nineteenth-century ballet repertory is another important focus of his theoretical writings in *The Ballet Master and His Art,* and one of the most fascinating aspects is his breakdown of step sequences in precise relationship to their music. Such detailed analysis is rare in the dance literature of any era, but it has an added value here in that it focuses on the sequences Lopukhov knew in the early twentieth century (assuming, of course, that his memory is accurate), and their documentation can aid in tracking choreographic changes over time. Many of these sequences have been captured since on film; some appear in notations from an earlier date (by Vladimir Stepanov, who devised the notation system used in Russia prior to the Revolution, Alexander Gorsky, Nicolas Sergeyev, and the latter's assistants Alexander Chekrygin and V. Rakhmanov), now part of the Sergeyev collection of notated classics housed in the Harvard Theatre Collection.[67] The versions Lopukhov knew date from the era of Sergeyev's régisseurship at the Maryinsky Theatre (1903–1918), but the notations, most of which date from 1898–1905, reveal textual discrepancies and editorial changes and suggest the existence of still earlier versions.[68]

One such example of choreographic change is the opening of Aurora's variation in Act III of *The Sleeping Beauty* (see p. 142–143 and music example 4). Lopukhov describes the Petipa choreography as follows: "In the first two semi-quavers of the first bar Petipa has the danseuse rise from fifth position to pointe on her right foot, with the left leg suspended in midair in an attitude effacé. During the next two semi-quavers she returns to fifth position with the other foot in front." In the second half of the bar, "he has the danseuse perform an almost exact repetition of the movements but starting with the other foot in front and with sur le cou-de-pied to the front in place of the attitude effacé." Lopukhov's point is that the advance "forward and to the side" of the first movement and the "upward progression" of the attitude effacé convey a statuesque quality and contour true to the music but that continuing with a similar kind of movement in the second half of the bar does not take into account the change to legato in the music. He considers that a turn would have been more appropriate at this point. In his analysis of the nineteenth-century repertory, Lopukhov was frequently critical of Petipa's musicality.

Other records of this moment suggest that "starting from the

Пример № ¡,14

Music example 4

other foot" in the second half of the bar really means "starting with the other foot in front." In the following analysis, I am assuming this interpretation. The Stepanov notation for this section indicates, for bar 1, relevé derrière with the right leg, close in fifth behind in plié, relevé passé with the right leg, close the right foot in fifth in front in plié; then, in bar 2, retaining the fifth position relationship, steps on pointe, right, left, and right. The pointe steps articulate the three repeating staccato notes in the melody in bar 2. The movement in bar 1 is clearly different from what Lopukhov knew. It is, however, much more like the version still danced by the Royal Ballet, which stems from the Sergeyev notes and his staging in 1939 for the then Vic-Wells Ballet (though sometimes the movement commences with the left as working leg, performed with the right when it repeats in bars 3–4).[69]

Lopukhov's description suggests that the choreography at the beginning of this variation had already changed in Russia by the time of *The Ballet Master and His Art*. Further changes took place during the Soviet period. Kirov/St. Petersburg and Bolshoi Ballet dancers customarily open the bar as Lopukhov describes but continue in the second half of the bar with a hop on the right leg as the left leg is extended into a petit développé devant. This is the version still performed by the Kirov Ballet today in the new production of 1999, publicized as a reconstruction from the Stepanov notations.[70] Again, three staccato steps on pointe follow in the second bar. Depending on the individual dancer's performance, the développé can create the more legato effect that Lopukhov recommended for the second half of bar 1. It is tempting to speculate that it might have been he who prompted the development. However, the simple repetition of the step combination described (on the other side of the body) while the music changes (bars 3–4) means that the established close relationship between music and dance does not continue.

Another of Lopukhov's examples from *The Sleeping Beauty* is the Waltz or Garland Dance from Act I (see p. 129). Here, the Stepanov notation, Lopukhov description, and recent Kirov productions are in agreement, except for minor details.[71] Lopukhov tells us that the Waltz begins with sixteen balancés to the musical melody, after a four-bar musical introduction. He rejects this response to the melody as mere "introductory" steps; the "dance proper" begins only after these sixteen bars. Recent Kirov productions, including the 1999 reconstruction, also show this balancé opening, the rows of couples progressing slowly toward the front of the stage. The early Stepanov notations indicate a step combination of two mazurka-style steps followed by two balancés. Again, it seems, a choreographic change had taken place by Lopukhov's time.

For the next sixteen-bar phrase, which begins with a repeat of the opening melody, a four-bar dance unit repeats four

times, the woman in each couple supported in an attitude
effacé, followed by step, pas de chat in front of her partner,
ending with a tendu croisé devant. Lopukhov regrets that the
change to hemiola rhythm from bar 9 in the musical phrase
is ignored: shifting from the conventional three-beat waltz
rhythm, "the melodic structure is based on two beats" until the
transitional bars 15–16 at the end of this phrase[72] (see music
example 5).

Пример № 12

Music example 5

Lopukhov mentions the return of balancés in the following
two bars (17–18), again a transitional movement rather than
the "proper" dance movement required here to demonstrate
the direct link between these bars and the new melody that
follows. He is correct in hearing these bars as a kind of upbeat
to the following melody. Both in the Stepanov notation and in
the recent Kirov productions, these steps begin earlier, during
the musical transition (bars 15–16), and continue through bars
17–18.[73] Lopukhov would have considered this appropriate, a
transitional passage in both music and choreography (bars 15–
16). But it is clear from his description that he remembered the
choreographic transition being delayed until the "upbeat" bars
17–18, in other words, until too late for musical sense. All versions are in agreement that there is no response to the sequence
of one-bar units that begins the next musical phrase (see fig.
13, p. 85), which Lopukhov, characteristically, regards as an
unfortunate miscalculation. The repeating dance unit is four
bars long: the women perform relevé in fifth position and then
fall to the side, supported by their partners.

Lopukhov analyzes Albrecht's variation in Act II of *Giselle* in its totality and with full diagrammatic representation (see p. 115). He traces problems from the very beginning, as Petipa fails to heed the change in the music between bars 1–2 and bars 3–4 and simply repeats the choreography of bars 1–2. "The double cabriole," writes Lopukhov, "which was a brilliant match for the semi-quavers of the first bar, was not at all appropriate for the third bar: whereas the first bar is stable, in the third bar the melody moves upward and proceeds in semi-quaver leaps that lend it a sparkling character." The curves of dance and music regularly diverge. "This," continues Lopukhov, "is particularly evident where the entrechat-six is performed in bars 2 and 6. The entrechat finishes (that is to say the dancer touches the ground) precisely at the point where the melody takes a sudden turn upward." Analyzing the rest of the variation, Lopukhov finds that, "in general, harmony and correspondence between music and dance are woefully lacking." His main quibble is with the mismatch of musical and dance "curves," which he considers typical of the age of "dance to the accompaniment of music."

Since Lopukhov's time, we have seen any number of different versions of this variation danced by different soloists (sometimes making decisions of their own) from different company traditions and on stages of different sizes (which can affect the number of repetitions of step combinations). There are always some similarities to the steps that Lopukhov describes. However, the most striking development is the shift from the regular format of three presentations of each step combination, followed by a transition, to a freer and more varied structure. There are no signs that establishing tighter relationships between choreographic and musical curves and thematic organization (variations, repetitions, and recapitulations) has become a priority.

Lopukhov also attends to relationships between movement and music in mime passages. He observes in connection with Carabosse's entrance in the Prologue of *The Sleeping Beauty* that Petipa gave the whole musical passage to Carabosse: "The King and Queen merely interrupt her to tell her that Catalabutte is very forgetful" (see p. 127). But Lopukhov hears the music in terms of Carabosse's angry triplets, periodic outbursts of rage, which break into a distinctive legato theme of appeasement, the King and Queen addressing Carabosse and begging her to forgive Catalabutte for not inviting her to the christening. Oddly, because we know that he had access to the musical score, Lopukhov does not mention that the dialogue he describes is clearly recorded in it as original intention. The score includes the words "La Roi et la Reine la supplient" (The King and Queen beg her to forgive). The same note is recorded, too, in Petipa's ballet master's plan and in the libretto for the ballet.

It is Petipa again that Lopukhov holds responsible—at least at the time of the treatise—for the lack of correspondence between mime and music in this passage; of all the artists he had seen performing Carabosse, only Alexander Chekrygin (not even the original Enrico Cecchetti) brought out the musical dialogue. Two points might be made here. First, Petipa allowed considerable interpretative freedom in mime passages, so the "error" might not have been his own. Lopukhov himself acknowledges this in his later writings.[74] Second, the loosening of the musical relationship could be part of a much broader tradition. As the music historian Marian Smith has pointed out, there has been a growing tendency during the history of both ballet and film for scores "to follow the characters' moods and motions less slavishly ... providing appropriate and suggestive music but eschewing the strict parallelism that had character-ized the earlier approach."[75] That tendency leads eventually to multivoiced texts and aural-visual dissonance. Roland John Wiley adds yet another strand to the argument, suggesting that Tchaikovsky himself was the first to admit that theater practice modifies original intentions: "From Marius Petipa he learned that you change as you go in ballet, as often as the circumstances warrant: only after collaboration can a theatre work be said to exist."[76] We can imagine a brilliant mime artist such as Cecchetti wanting to take the Carabosse scene on his own terms, even rereading the legato theme of appeasement as a darker, power-building representation of himself.[77] Recent productions have tended toward a freer musical response than Lopukhov permits, still keeping the attention regularly on Carabosse—all, that is, except the reconstruction by the mime specialist Giannandrea Poesio. Poesio matches gestures more closely to the dialogue structure and the semiotic content of the music.[78]

Despite his criticisms of Petipa's musicality, Lopukhov undertook the restoration of nine Petipa ballets during his career, six of them during the early 1920s, and there is little evidence that he changed their fundamental musicality. Lopukhov's main goal was to restore cuts made by Petipa from the original Tchaikovsky scores (cuts for which he chastises Petipa) and to create new choreography for these passages in Petipa style. One passage from the nineteenth-century repertory that he did "correct" musically was Ivanov's Waltz of the Snowflakes in *The Nutcracker* (see p. 65). "The Snowflakes scene" he writes, "is devoid of harmony, lacks development, and is ill-conceived from the point of view of the placing of musical themes. Figures that change after every eight bars do not work for the whole of the Waltz of the Snowflakes."[79]

In his later years, Lopukhov revised his ideas about Petipa's musicality, not only approving as innovative his use of sonata form but also deciding that *The Sleeping Beauty* is, after all, a fine setting of the music. He again makes the point (for which he had criticized Petipa in his treatise) that "choreographers should understand that movement which only keeps to the general meter cannot be called musical." But, only a sentence later, bemoaning the fact that "choreographers are not always masters of intonation in dance, which should be in harmony with the music," he proclaims boldly that "this insufficiency is not to be found in Petipa's *The Sleeping Beauty*."[80] Likewise, Petipa is innocent with regard to *Swan Lake*. Now, Lopukhov charges the composer-conductor, Riccardo Drigo, with full responsibility for the cutting of Tchaikovsky's score.[81]

So why Lopukhov's so different early opinions, some of which could now be seen as narrow, pedantic, and even eccentric?

First, we must recognize that Lopukhov was writing with passionate commitment at a time when the fundamental tenets of dance and dance music were undergoing radical change. Perhaps, too, it was in Lopukhov's interests in the early twentieth century to side to some degree with the strong anti-Petipa faction of the era's Left[82] and to emphasize the need for improving on past practice. And perhaps the issue of structural integration of media was not so pressing by midcentury as it had been during the heyday of Dalcroze in the 1910s and 1920s. We might speculate that Lopukhov felt a certain pressure to theorize unity—unity of choreographic form, or "symphonism," as well as unity between music and dance—during the period 1916–1925 when *The Ballet Master and His Art* was written. This could have been a consoling aesthetic standpoint in a period of political turmoil; it was a position that found favor with a number of other artists at the time, not least too because it meant exploring the essential materials of the medium, a key feature of modernism.

Lopukhov presents a linear view of history in his treatise: he subscribes to the principle of gradual progress from an earlier practice that provided for no correspondence between music and dance to a new ideal of synthesis, from nineteenth-century rhythmic dissonance and patchwork choreography to twentieth-century symphonic schemes of true structural integration. Little did he know that there were precedents for dance "symphonism" and visualization of musical structure that dated from before Petipa's time. Sandra Hammond, for instance, has identified a number of examples in the choreographic notebooks compiled by Michel St. Léon between 1829 and 1836: examples of choreographic theme and variation structure interweaving with a corresponding musical structure.[83] We can extend still further back in history to the numerous *Folies d'Espagne* of the early eighteenth century, each of these a series of choreographic variations. Then, too, in the sixteenth century, the galliard exemplified variation structure in both music and dance.[84] However, to Lopukhov, art progressed, gradually and simply, in one direction—forward.

After the 1920s, as Lopukhov himself recognized, theorists of music and dance were no longer so fiercely consistent in demanding structural parallelism. There was, if anything, a shift *backward* to a looser approach. Doris Humphrey and Balanchine have shown that such an approach can still encourage audiences to listen to the music while watching the dance. More recently, Mark Morris has made us look again sympathetically at the tighter "mickey-mouse" relationship. Art practices do not develop simply in one direction.

Yet, from the standpoint of his own period, Lopukhov undeniably occupies an important position in the history of choreographic theory. Balanchine (who was directly influenced by Lopukhov), Léonide Massine, Frederick Ashton, and Twyla Tharp are but a few of the many choreographers who, since the 1920s, have taken up the challenges of dance symphonism, of choreography that relies neither on story nor theatricality, and of sophisticated interaction with music.

The Ballet Master and His Art

Contents of *The Ballet Master and His Art*

The following list of contents of *The Ballet Master and His Art* locates the chapters selected for translation within the book as a whole. There is a brief explanation of the contents of each chapter, as well as a summary guide to those that follow. Translated chapters are followed by an asterisk.

Part 1: The Evolution of Choreography

1. Noverre and Viganò [A comparison of their traditions and a proposal that their opposing principles should be combined.]
2. The Ballet Master and the Score* [Advocating the necessity for choreographers to undertake study of the full musical score.]
3. The "Soft" versus the "Hard" Plié [An outline of the features of classical dance (based on the soft plié) and character dance (based on the hard plié).]
4. A Third Category: the "Grotesque" [A discussion of body types suited to the different forms of dance, the form of the future containing elements of all choreographic ideas to date and requiring a new body shape and new movements.]
5. The Dance Symphony* [A plea for the development of dance as an autonomous art form. An outline of the *Dance Symphony* on the theme "The Magnificence of the Universe" (used in slightly modified order in the final 1923 work), with the comment that, ideally, the music should be composed specifically to suit the dance. There is no mention of using Beethoven's Fourth Symphony.]

6. Dance Symphonism* [Advocating the principle of choreographic thematic development. The ideal is symphonism in
both music and dance (this links with the next chapter).]

Part 2: The Position of Dance in Relation to Music: Separate, Dominant, Subordinate, and Integrated [Four stages in
the relationship between music and dance are proposed. The
fourth stage is the ideal, and Lopukhov outlines the characteristics of this stage. The chapter includes analysis of sections of
Giselle, which is an example of a simple score in general effectively choreographed, while he considers Petipa's *The Sleeping
Beauty* "set to" Tchaikovsky's music as not rising to the challenge of its complexity. There are musical examples from both
Giselle and *Beauty,* with graphic analysis of excerpts from *Giselle*
to demonstrate complementary spatial/pitch curves in the dance
and music. Lopukhov considers the danger of the Dalcroze
approach as being too mechanical.]

Part 3: Ethnic Dance Movements
1. Introduction [The thesis of part 3 is that the physical features of a region such as mountains or plains affect the gait
of its inhabitants and are consequently reflected in the
dances of that region. Classical dance can exist only where
all signs of nationality have been obliterated, that is to say
in cities, and classical dance is classless and international.
Lopukhov seeks to justify the claim that, in order to stage
ethnic dances successfully, it is vital to study the physical
characteristics of their country of origin.]
2. Ethnic Dance Movements and the *Polovtsian Dances* as
staged by Michel Fokine and Lev Ivanov [Lopukhov gives
as an example of his thesis the case of Fokine, who knew
the steppes and understood that the wide open spaces
were reflected in the movement of the Polovtsians. Ivanov
did not understand this point.]
3. The Ethnic Dance Movements of Egypt
4. The Ethnic Dance Movements of Great Russia
5. The Ethnic Dance Movements of Little Russia

Conclusion* [This section includes statements that suggest that it (at least) was written after the Revolution. Lopukhov says that the authorities seem to believe that choreography is a bourgeois-capitalist activity, unnecessary and alien to the proletariat, but that they should recognize that classical ballet choreography in its most refined form of the dance symphony is classless and international. The art of choreography is being reborn. The Revolution has not damaged it. We must not allow it to stagnate.]

A Note about Dating

In *Sixty Years in Ballet* (243), Lopukhov states that he began writing *The Ballet Master and His Art* in 1916, and, indeed, there is much evidence to suggest that there was a time gap in the writing process before publication in 1925. The sharp break in content between part 3 and parts 1 and 2 support this thesis, as well as the discrepancies that arise from a reading, after parts 1 and 2, of the Conclusion.

In parts 1 and 2, there is no reference to Lopukhov's own work on restoring the classics in 1922 and 1923, which would be odd had he written these sections in the mid-1920s. Nor does he mention his choice of Beethoven or his staging of *Dance Symphony* in 1922. Indeed, no choreography is mentioned that postdates Fokine's 1913 ballet *Les Préludes*. The fact that Lopukhov does not mention any of the Fokine ballets of 1915 and 1916, that in *Sixty Years* (243) he acknowledges having seen, is surprising and suggests an even earlier commencement date for the treatise. At the beginning of part 2, he writes that "the idea of treating dance and music as one is very new: it was first put forward less than five years ago." Here he is most likely referring to the advent of Dalcroze eurhythmics in the early 1910s (see introduction). It would have made no sense for Lopukhov to refer to "the idea of treating dance and music as one" as new in 1920.

Three comments in parts 1 and 2 suggest later updating. There is a reference in part 1, chapter 2, to Igor Glebov's *Symphonic Studies* of 1922 and in chapter 5 to Lopukhov's 1922 article on Isadora Duncan, "Moi Otvet." In part 2, Lopukhov refers disparagingly to a work staged to Debussy by an experimental choreographer, possibly the Moscow-based Kasian Goleizovsky, whose Chamber Ballet performed in Petrograd in 1922, including *Faun* on its program (to Debussy's *Prélude à l'après-midi d'un faune*).

The conclusion is utterly unambiguous as to its postrevolutionary date. Lopukhov writes in passionate defense of the classical tradition, obviously feeling anxious about the prospects for its survival, an anxiety for which there was cause in the immediate postrevolutionary period. He also refers to the offering of free ballet tickets to Soviet workers after the Revolution. Nevertheless, Lopukhov sees himself as part of the way forward within the terms of the new Soviet régime, a modernist reacting against "a romanticism that is now played out." He refers to the swift pace of events "of the past fifteen or twenty years," surely referring to the period that began with the first revolution of 1905 or with Isadora Duncan's first performances in Russia in 1904.

Translator's Note

The Ballet Master and His Art is a passionate manifesto in support of choreography. Lopukhov's writing is characterized by great vigor and enthusiasm; it also has a rather informal tone, so that the reader feels that he or she is being addressed "live" by a speaker who is intermittently carried away by his subject. The style of the work is attractive because it makes the reader feel acquainted with the writer as a person, but it does pose certain problems for the translator. The main difficulties are a consequence of the "stream-of-consciousness" nature of the prose. Paragraphs are often of unmanageable length; sentences are sometimes long and rambling; there are numerous repetitions. The line of argument is not always clear: the writer digresses, then digresses from the digression, then returns to his original theme without making clear connections between the points he has covered. The use of terms is not always consistent. For example, the names of ballet steps are sometimes in correct French, sometimes in incorrect French, and sometimes in Russian.

My aim in translating this work has been to produce an English version that is as accurate as possible but at the same time conveys Lopukhov's enthusiasm and is accessible and attractive to the modern reader. To this end, I have departed from the original text in a number of ways. I have broken the work into shorter paragraphs and broken very long sentences into shorter ones. Where there are repetitions in consecutive sentences I have condensed two sentences into one. Where the line of argument has not been clear, in the English version I have endeavored to make it more so (e.g., by using an appropriate noun in place of an ambiguous pronoun, or by referring back to a previous key phrase in order to make a connection), while at the same time remaining true to the meaning of the Russian text. I have attempted to use terms clearly and consistently unless the Russian version is genuinely vague.

This approach makes the English version "faster" than it would have been without the changes described; however, I believe that the result is easier to read and more likely to appeal to its intended audience. Most important, I have done my best to recreate the tone and the spirit of the original.

Dorinda Offord

Editor's Note

Lopukhov's musical examples and accompanying diagrams have been reproduced here in facsimile. Lopukhov adopts the five-line stave from music for showing the lines of both musical pitch contour and rise and fall in the level of the dance, one stave for each line, the music above the dance, and both lines below the music in piano reduction. Perhaps he was inclined to adopt the musical model because he turned to music so frequently for his conceptual framework. He also uses musical repeat signs for repeating step units. Lopukhov treats the diagrammatic principles with a degree of freedom. For instance, a circle indicates a turn (not a circular pathway in a vertical plane). Then, as step units are repeated down the diagonal of the stage, the level of movement line rises, not that the dancer's level literally rises, but the line is presumably intended to give the impression of increasing energy and dynamic excitement.

Lopukhov's original notes appear as footnotes; all others appear as endnotes.

The Ballet Master and the Score

Until very recently, it was inconceivable that a ballet master past or present might be interested in the musical score of the ballet he was required to stage. And yet, once the great composers withdrew their self-imposed ban on writing music for the ballet (an art they had previously regarded as second-rate), it became essential for ballet masters not simply to take an interest in the score prior to staging the ballet but to study it in depth. As Igor Glebov in his *Symphonic Studies* explains, until 1889 it never occurred to Russian composers that a form of art that was so despised might be capable of bringing such glory to the Russian arts in general, or that the considerable talents of Russia's finest musicians would be devoted to ballet.[1]

The first composer to write music specifically for ballet was Tchaikovsky. In agreeing to do so, he was not simply bowing to the demands of Prince Vsevolozhsky, the then director of the former Imperial Theaters.[2] Rather, as an exponent of another art form—music—he must have been aware of a number of important points, namely:

1. that choreography in the form of ballet is a most exalted art, at least on a level with the other arts;
2. that the sphere of ballet music offered an enormous opportunity to him as a composer;
3. that dance rhythms in general are of considerable significance in Slavonic music;
4. that ballet is still in its infancy with its golden age yet to

come, since for a variety of reasons it has developed as an
art form far more slowly than other art forms;

5. that the inferior status of ballet and the reluctance of
   composers to write music for it continue to delay its
   development.

These, I believe, are the considerations that persuaded Tchaikovsky to compose music for ballet. His decision to do so constitutes a major step forward. *The Sleeping Beauty* demonstrated
that it is by no means beneath the dignity of a composer to
write music for ballet. And, ever since then, it has been vital for
the ballet master to study the music score in detail.

In order to make it clear why I attach such importance to this
turning point, it is necessary to look back into the past and to
examine the ways in which ballet music was formerly created.
We need not consider the period before Petipa, since Petipa
himself worked according to rules laid down long before and
for many years regarded as unshakable. In any case, at that time
people did not pay as much attention to the music of a ballet
as they do now. The order of events in the creation of a ballet
used to be as follows: first of all, the story line would be established (in those days that was the only element of which anyone could be certain), then the narrative would be scanned
for a part or role for a main character (usually the ballerina). In
consultation with her, it would then be decided how many
entrances, adagios, variations, codas, and other dances designed
to show her off to best advantage her part should contain. At
this point, in order to ensure that the main character should
have the chance to rest and also in order to make the performance longer, it would be necessary to insert a few processions
and large-scale waltzes that had nothing whatsoever to do with
the story, and also a few extra pas de deux for persons lower in
rank than the ballerina but nevertheless important for some
reason. As far as the music was concerned, there was always a
home-grown writer of tunes on hand whose job it was to write
what he was told to write, bearing in mind only the style of

the dances of this or that character. If the result proved unsatisfactory from the point of view of its correspondence with the dance, the matter was easily dealt with: the offending variation was simply dropped and replaced by a variation from an existing ballet.[a] The new ballet was not affected in any way by these insertions, nor did it lose its musical character, since the variations inserted from ballets written previously had themselves been devised in the way I have just described and by the same writer of tunes.

There is a story about the famous "bookshelves" of one such music writer who was under contract to the theater management to write two ballets a year. The nature of these bookshelves was curious and instructive for those who wrote the music for ballets in the past. Each shelf was labeled: waltzes, marches, variations, and so on. It may be argued that there is nothing wrong or even unusual about this; after all, every composer has a stock of musical sketches. However, such an argument would only be partially justifiable. Sketches of this nature usually relate to specific subject matter. An artist works in a similar way: after he has identified the subject matter for a picture, he makes a series of sketches before embarking upon the picture itself. However, in the case of ballet composers, the situation was rather different. The product of their creativity was not sketches of marches, waltzes, or variations appropriate to specific subject matter but simply ready-made pieces of music—marches, waltzes, and variations—that could be placed on the relevant shelf in the expectation that sooner or later they would be needed. And inevitably they *would* be needed, since, in accordance with the contract, two new ballets had to be written every year.

Once the resident music writer had been informed of the newly created story line for a ballet, the bookshelves really came into their own. All the waltzes, marches, and variations were taken down, and from their number were selected those deemed

a. This is still a common practice in old-style ballets.

most suitable, without any consideration of the possibility that the style of these marches and all the rest might not be appropriate. When this was done, the music was regarded as more or less finished, and, if it became necessary to make any additions, there would be no problem. Of course, I do not wish to imply that all composers working for the theater management acted thus, but there is clear evidence to corroborate the story of the "bookshelves." As a consequence of the practice I have described, the majority of the older ballets have virtually identical music, and within ballets there is rarely any consistency of musical style. I do not hold the composers themselves responsible, as they were answerable to the ballet master and the main character, and, more important, they were the product of an age that demanded nothing more of ballet performances than a series of charming numbers. Audiences did not look for the choreographic embodiment of an idea; all they wanted was a pleasant relaxing spectacle or a tour de force, since for most people ballet was merely a way of passing time. What dark days choreography has lived through, and how wonderful that those days are now only a memory! It is hardly surprising that leading musicians refused to have anything to do with this type of work, since it required slavish subordination to the vulgar tastes of the public, which, though outwardly "cultured," was in fact totally undiscriminating. The fact that the commissioned ranks were sent to Glinka's opera *Ruslan and Ludmila* by way of punishment is some indication of the kind of taste dominant at that time.[4]

Obviously, the great composers were not really of the opinion that ballet had no right to recognition as a form of choreographic art. This is particularly clear from the example of Glinka's *Ruslan and Ludmila*: ballet plays an important part in the opera, and yet the music is written without any concessions to popular taste. And then there is Rimsky-Korsakov, who did not write any ballets but who created the opera-ballet *Mlada*,[5] more than half of which actually consists of ballet: surely that indicates a recognition of ballet as a form of high art. In short, the question is not whether composers accepted ballet as such but whether they were prepared to accept the views and tastes that prevailed at the time and have not disappeared completely even today. Tchaikovsky's belief in ballet as art must have been very strong if, in spite of the circumstances I have just described, he nevertheless resolved to compose *The Sleeping Beauty* in the face of prevailing taste.

Having explained the reasons why composers were unwilling to compose music for ballet, I shall continue my analysis of the ballet master's role before Tchaikovsky's time from the stage at which a new ballet first went into rehearsal. I should first of all draw the reader's attention to one important point. With a few rare exceptions, neither the ballet master nor the conductor ever saw the full score in advance, for the simple reason that it did not exist. All the work was done to a répétiteur[6]—a version of the music scored for one or two violins on the basis of which scenes, dances, and orchestral parts were devised. To those who are unfamiliar with the ways of ballet, this may seem absurd, all the more so because normal practice in the course of staging an opera is in effect the reverse: to derive the individual orchestral parts from the full score. However, ballet proceeded along completely different lines, and, in the vast majority of cases, the music was written from the outset as individual parts, without there ever being a full score. There is an enormous difference between earlier methods of writing music and modern orchestration. An analysis of this difference is beyond the scope of this work, but certain aspects of it are of some relevance to our present theme, and for this reason I shall consider it in greater detail.

Whoever wrote down the ballet music for the orchestra— whether the composer himself or someone else to whom the task had been assigned—was bound by the rule that really mattered for ballet at that time: to wit, that all of the composer's work must sound exactly the same when played by a full orchestra as it would in rehearsal. Typically, the répétiteur always followed the same principle: it was scored for two instruments, two violins. The first violin would play the melody, the second an accompaniment, while the piano would join in to reinforce both the melody and the accompaniment.[7] Thus works were rehearsed to the accompaniment of a sort of mini-orchestra. For a full orchestral performance, a musical transcriber would blindly reproduce the répétiteur: he would give the melody to the first violins, reinforcing it with the woodwind in unison; the accompaniment, which was very simple, would go to the second violins and the violas, reinforced by the bass strings and the brass. Thus, the orchestra was divided into two halves, one playing the melody in unison, the other the accompaniment, with the addition of drums at emotional high points. All ballets of the time were performed against a similar orchestral background. Perhaps I should not say all, but the vast majority, as there were exceptions, even fine ones, though good exceptions were few and far between.

So, did the ballet master who was staging a ballet at that time really need the score? Of course not. Even if he had had it in front of him, he would have gained nothing from familiarity with it, since the only difference between a performance of the music by the rehearsal trio and the full orchestral performance consisted in the fact that the latter was several times louder. The ballet master creating an entrance or variation could unerringly reproduce in the performance the same mood as had been created in rehearsal, since he could be absolutely certain that the first violins would be playing the theme and would dominate, so that the mood would be determined by the sound of the violins. The same is no longer true; nowadays the theme is played on a piano in rehearsal, whereas in the orchestral version it might be played by an oboe. This, of course, is extremely important, since each instrument has its own characteristics and timbre. Movements that are devised to match a mood created by the sound of a violin will certainly not be appropriate if executed to the accompaniment of a bassoon. I find that a single musical theme takes on a completely different character depending upon whether it is played by a violin, an oboe, or another instrument, purely as a consequence of the instrument's characteristics. Hence, if a particular theme recurs within a ballet but is played on different occasions by different instruments, there must be corresponding differences in the choreography. The basic idea, of course, remains, as does the musical theme, but the mood of the performance must change. In short, the different colors and timbres of the different instruments must be reflected in the choreography as well. This is the only way to achieve the desirable harmony between music and choreography.

In the age when ballet music was performed by an orchestra playing the melody in unison against a simple accompaniment,[8] the whole question of instrumental timbre could be largely ignored. If, in the course of a performance, thunder or some other manifestation of a natural phenomenon was required, it was reproduced offstage by purely realistic means. The impression of actual thunder would be conveyed, but the possibility of suggesting thunder musically was never even considered. (In this instance, a bravura march might have served the purpose.) Nowadays, however, the orchestra has come into its own, and it is impossible to imagine what the orchestral performance of a work will sound like on the basis of the piano score alone. Post-Tchaikovsky attempts to stage ballets purely on the basis of the piano score are doomed: there is a risk of error in virtually every bar in terms of both mood and timbre, and the result is the destruction of the harmony of which I spoke earlier and which is so essential to choreography.

Let me cite an example that provides a graphic illustration of the point I am making. When Vladimir Telyakovsky was director of the former Imperial Theaters,[9] he conceived the idea of reorchestrating the music for the ballet *La Bayadère,* which was originally written by Ludwig Minkus and was generally thought to be more or less acceptable. Boris Asafiev was commissioned to carry out the reorchestration.[10] The idea of reorchestration is admirable in itself, but, given that the music in question was ballet music, the whole undertaking merely served to illuminate the failure to understand the difference between the old-style melody-and-accompaniment music and the new-style orchestration. For Telyakovsky, a man generally considered to be musically educated, Nicholas Sergeyev, his chief producer, and Alexander Monakhov, the leader of the company,[11] allowed

La Bayadère to go to performance with new orchestration but without making any choreographic changes whatsoever. There were some comic incidents at the first rehearsal with the orchestra: apart from the fact that no one recognized the music, for some reason all the dancers were out of time, with the result that it looked as though Petipa had choreographed the ballet very badly, with complete disregard for rhythm. Everyone knew that timing had never been a problem with the old orchestration, yet suddenly with the new orchestration the most crass errors had crept in, of a sort that had never occurred before in any of Petipa's productions, not even the least successful. The harmony between the dance and its orchestral accompaniment had been lost once and for all. Where previously a solemn section in the music had been reflected by a solemn section in the dance, with the new orchestration virtually the opposite was the case.

Many people blamed the dancers for this failure, accusing them of being "cloth-eared." However, these accusations were undoubtedly misdirected, since the performers faithfully followed all Petipa's directions, which had never caused difficulties with rhythm before. Others claimed that Asafiev was at fault, that in changing the music he had departed from the original. Yet Asafiev had carried out his task in accordance with all the latest principles of orchestration. I sat in on a rehearsal at that time, and it became abundantly clear to me that, in order to stage a ballet, it was vital to study the full score. Monakhov argued that ignorance of the new orchestration was the cause of the poor performances and that, after a few rehearsals, when the dancers had had a chance to familiarize themselves with it, harmony between the music and the choreography would be restored. In fact, however, this was further proof of his failure to understand the nature of the new-style orchestration. Reorchestration demands a restaging of the entire ballet and the creation of a new piano score that will convey to performers an accurate impression of the new sound of the music. Bitter experience has thus clearly demonstrated the need to study the full score of the latest composers. For the time being, Minkus's original orchestration has been reinstated for all performances of *La Bayadère.*

From the moment when the music of the best composers began to accompany ballet, the famous trio of first and second violins plus piano began to disappear from rehearsals. It clung to its role from Tchaikovsky's to Fokine's day on the strength of tradition, but rigor mortis had already set in, for no trio can successfully recreate for the purposes of ballet an accurate impression of the orchestration, color, and resonance of the music of Tchaikovsky and the composers who came after him. Petipa did not realize this: as far as he was concerned, it was possible to treat Tchaikovsky in the same way as previous composers of ballet music. Of course, Petipa cannot be blamed for his attitude: he was trained exclusively on the basis of old principles, and it is obvious that it never occurred to him that Tchaikovsky's music might raise some new questions in relation to ballet. But one has only to compare ballets to music by the old composers with ballets to the music of Tchaikovsky to understand the difference. If we look at those productions by Petipa that predate Tchaikovsky, we rarely find errors in relation to the simple melody-and-accompaniment music of the time. The mood of this or that character is always closely associated with the musical accompaniment. As for the rhythm, which in those days was very uncomplicated by comparison with present-day rhythm, there is likewise no mismatch, thanks to the fact that the rehearsal trio conveyed a totally accurate impression of the mood, rhythm, and resonance of the full orchestral version of the music.

Petipa was the leading ballet maker of the previous epoch, and his talent dominated ballet music. His word was law, and on his orders any variation or entrance could be instantly rejected and replaced by another one. Partly because he had grown accustomed to the subordination of ballet musicians and partly because ballet musicians were in any case at a lower stage of musical development than he was, Petipa, like his predecessors, was of the firm opinion that the music that accompanies ballet should be dependent upon the wishes of the ballet master and that it could be endlessly chopped up. Ballet masters did not imagine that one day a composer would appear who was not subordinate to them but would work in conjunction with them, nor were they aware that the outrageous cuts they made, which deprived music of all its meaning, were quite unacceptable. In short, in the opinion of ballet masters of Petipa's time and before, the function of music was to accompany the performance of a ballet, not to work together with it. How wrong they were. Dance without music is dead; if the music is subordinated to the dance, it trails along behind, and that contact which is possible only when dance and music are of equal importance is inevitably lost.

It was with this misguided view of the role of ballet music that Petipa started work on *The Sleeping Beauty*. He could not see that Tchaikovsky was no Pugni or Minkus. We have just recently begun to approach Tchaikovsky's work with some caution, because people have just recently begun to realize that there is more to his ballet music than a series of charming little tunes. And yet, not so long ago that was precisely how it was regarded, and only a study of Tchaikovsky's entire oeuvre has forced us toward a more complimentary evaluation. Petipa, approaching *The Sleeping Beauty* with the attitudes dominant at that time, inevitably made mistakes, both because he failed to understand the music as a whole and because he interpreted individual musical themes incorrectly; consequently, the whole production is wrong. The rehearsal trio could not accurately convey the mood or instrumentation of *The Sleeping Beauty*, and, as a result, this production, unlike any of Petipa's previous productions, conspicuously lacked any correspondence between music and dance. I do not share the view that Petipa's ballets to the music of Tchaikovsky are his greatest achievement. On the contrary, I find that they are full of errors not to be found in his ballets to the music of Tchaikovsky's predecessors. It was only thanks to his genuine talent, by which he was intuitively guided, that he was able to stage Tchaikovsky's ballets in ignorance of the score without completely ruining them.

Petipa was obviously aware that there was a problem, because for Tchaikovsky's subsequent ballets he collaborated with the ballet master Lev Ivanov. However, even this collaboration did not produce any better results, for the same reason: unwillingness to study the full score. And yet only the full score could properly convey Tchaikovsky's ideas; only the full score could give a true impression of the sonority of his orchestration. The prevailing view of music as subordinate to ballet justified Petipa's decision to cut and abbreviate the music; in my opinion, this amounts to blasphemy against Tchaikovsky, in whose music nothing is superfluous and every single bar flows from the previous one, forming an integral part of the whole work. Some might point out that the cuts were actually made by Tchaikovsky himself; however, we should not forget that Tchaikovsky was of mild character: when persistent pressure was put on him to make cuts and substitutions, he complied simply for the sake of peace, though no doubt such pestering was extraordinarily irksome to him. This is evident from the fact that eventually, even though convinced that cuts and partial changes deprived his work of meaning and value, he still allowed it to be completely lacerated.[12] *The Sleeping Beauty* is not distorted beyond recognition, it is true, but even such distortion as there is is an insult to Tchaikovsky's work. It was utterly improper to ask Tchaikovsky to write a new variation for Aurora in Act II, but he agreed even to that. Only when one looks at the original version does it become obvious that the first variation is far more consistent with the spirit of the act as a whole. How it must have pained Tchaikovsky to relinquish it! It is easy to see why all the added musical numbers and variations, such as Cinderella's scene in the last act, seem so different from the rest of *The Sleeping Beauty*. Indeed, Tchaikovsky himself honestly admitted that he was following orders for which he had little enthusiasm.[13]

The weakest section of *The Sleeping Beauty* is undoubtedly the part where Aurora and the Nereids appear to Prince Florimund in Act II.[14] The lightness and radiance of Aurora's appearance, the birth of Florimund's love for her, the luminosity of the

background, and then the joyful moment before her disappear-
ance into the forest are staged by Petipa in a manner that is at
variance with that dictated by the full score. I am sure that if
Petipa, with all his talent, had taken the time to familiarize
himself with the score, he would have staged the ballet quite
differently. There is no doubt that the rehearsal trio did not
convey a true impression of the Vision Scene. In those sections,
where the trio did succeed in producing a more or less accurate
imitation of the orchestral sound, Petipa achieved the most
magnificent harmony between music and dance. The dance of
the Blue Bird, for example, is in my opinion faultless as far as
its relationship to the music is concerned. (It opens with the
embodiment of the lightness of flight to the sound of a flute
and ends with a splendid masculine coda representing a bird
hovering.)

On a superficial level, the mistakes Petipa made in this production are barely noticeable, since the music of *The Sleeping
Beauty* makes one forget them. But, if for the purpose of comparison, we consider the ballet *Les Caprices du Papillon* (with
music by Nikolai Krotkov),[15] which Petipa staged before *The
Sleeping Beauty*, we find that the interpretation of the music and
the correspondence between music and dance are almost perfect—unlike *The Sleeping Beauty*, where the music is obviously
misinterpreted and the dances do not match the music except
in a few rare instances. In all fairness, it must be said that these
few instances where there *is* a close harmony between music
and dance suggest that a successful staging of *The Sleeping
Beauty* was well within Petipa's competence. He possessed a
boundless imagination within the field of dance, and only his
blind faith in the rehearsal trio prevented him from carrying
out his work impeccably.

Petipa relinquished sole responsibility for Tchaikovsky's second ballet, *The Nutcracker*, staging it jointly with Lev Ivanov.[16]
I use the phrase "relinquish responsibility" advisedly: Petipa
was generally too independent to tolerate the presence of a collaborator. Moreover, he occupied an exceptionally influential
position, and, had he so wished, he could easily have refused to

allow Ivanov to stage a single ballet. There were certainly instances where Petipa did make his influence felt in this way. It
is a well-known fact that the choreographic talents of Ivanov,
whose creative period coincided with that of Petipa, were not
used to the full. Thus, the only possible explanation for Petipa's
decision to collaborate with Ivanov is that, in *The Sleeping
Beauty*, he became acutely aware of the problems Tchaikovsky's
music posed for him.[17] Indeed, the collaboration between
Petipa and Ivanov is only to be seen in ballets to the music of
Tchaikovsky. However, their collaboration on *The Nutcracker*
did not, in fact, yield positive results. The score of *The Nutcracker* is considerably more difficult than the score of *The
Sleeping Beauty*. We can say with certainty that, even now, there
may be arguments over its interpretation, so fresh does it
remain. But Petipa and Ivanov persisted in working along the
old lines, not studying the score but relying entirely on the
mood created by the performance of the rehearsal trio, and, of
course, given the greater complexity of the score of *The Nutcracker*, there were even more errors. I do not wish to enter
into a discussion of whether Petipa and Ivanov actually understood the music of *The Nutcracker*. (I am inclined to think they
did not: virtually everything points in that direction.) Instead,
I shall confine myself to an analysis of what is pertinent to the
theme of the present chapter—the timbre of the orchestration
and the harmony between dance and music.

The Snowflakes scene is devoid of harmony, lacks development, and is ill conceived from the point of view of the placing
of musical themes. Figures that change after every eight bars
do not work for the whole of the Waltz of the Snowflakes. The
chorus singing in the wings is completely disregarded. If I am
at pains to emphasize the faults in the Waltz of the Snowflakes,
it is for the simple reason that many people think that it is wonderful. I do not agree; I believe that Ivanov's staging is actually
antimusical.

I do not even think it worthwhile to analyze Act II. Absolutely everything is wrong, with the exception of a few individual pas de deux and the Sugar Plum Fairy variation, which is

beautifully executed from the point of view of the harmony between the dance and the music. This is understandable: the variation is played by a glockenspiel in the orchestral version and by the piano at rehearsals so that a similar mood and timbre is present both at rehearsal and in performance.

When we come to *Swan Lake,* the first task is to put the score in order. Not one of the older ballets has been subjected to so many changes and cuts. One has the impression that Petipa and Ivanov had lost confidence in Tchaikovsky's first two ballets and, together with the conductor, Drigo, decided to reassemble this third ballet in a completely different order, treating it as Tchaikovsky's least successful ballet to date. We find not only that numerous cuts have been made but also that many of the dances have been moved. Only Act II is good: it is staged in Petipa's favorite tones, like the second act of *Giselle* and the Shades scene in *La Bayadère.*[18] But ignorance of the full score is apparent from the first entrance of the Swan Queen. In the orchestral version, Tchaikovsky gives the mournful theme depicting the metamorphosis of the girl into a swan at the hands of an evil genius to an oboe, an instrument ideally suited to the expression of sorrow and suppressed longing. Petipa's choreography is of a different character. It is sorrowful, but not as sorrowful as the oboe. It is sad in the way that the sound of a violin is sad. Again, this is a consequence of the fact that the staging was carried out on the basis of the mood conveyed by a violin—a false mood created by that same old rehearsal trio. Petipa was as unfamiliar with the orchestral score of *Swan Lake* as he was with the scores of the previous Tchaikovsky ballets. But this ballet convinces me that the correct staging was well within Petipa's capabilities, for, in rehearsal, where this section was played by a violin with piano accompaniment,[19] the impression was one of total harmony between music and choreography.

In ballets to the music of Alexander Glazunov, which acquire an endless variety of brilliant colors in orchestral performance, failure to study the score is even more apparent. Where musical themes flit magically from one instrument to another, the total lack of correspondence between the dance and the music is particularly noticeable. A good example is the stick dance in the second act of *Raymonda:* there is no correspondence between music and dance either in the rhythm (except at the very beginning) or in the layout of material, or in the allocation of choreographic movements to the musical material, or in their development. The same is true of the dream scene, apart from the variations. (I have singled out only the most obvious instances.) On the other hand, in those sections where Petipa knew for certain which instrument in the orchestra would be playing the musical theme, and especially when this was a solo (for example, Raymonda's variation in the dream scene, her variation in the last act, and her second-act coda), he achieved brilliant results, both in the staging per se and in the correspondence between staging and music. I will never cease to regret the fact that Petipa never managed to look at the full score. What exquisite harmony and correspondence between music and dance he could have achieved!

It is still the case today that ballet masters start work without first studying the score. Even Fokine's ballets contain passages that make it clear that he had not looked at the score beforehand. But Fokine, being possessed of a high degree of musical sensitivity, always treated the music properly on the basis of intuition and instinctively extrapolated the true color and timbre of the orchestration from the piano version alone (the famous rehearsal trio was by this time finally defunct). Incidently, it is curious that everyone should have acknowledged the superfluity of the rehearsal trio, whereas the need to study the score is still obvious to only a few. I know that, before starting work on any production of a ballet, Fokine played the music countless times on the piano. As a result, he was able to absorb and correctly define the color and timbre of the orchestration. However, one can repeat a piece on the piano far more times than Fokine did and still be incapable of imagining the orchestral version. If, on the other hand, one studies the score, such time wasting becomes unnecessary, and one knows without having to guess how the orchestra will sound.[b]

I have endeavored to show that studying the score makes it infinitely easier for a ballet master to stage a ballet. A knowledge of the score helps to bring about that marvelous harmony between music and dance that is so essential to the art of choreography. Therefore, I conclude this chapter with a plea to ballet masters to study their scores thoroughly before embarking upon the production of a ballet and to have them at hand at all times when they are working. By this means they can guarantee that the art of choreography will succeed and thrive.

b. Fokine still leads the field in this respect; his latest works were all staged *after* he had studied the score.

The Dance Symphony

It is obvious to me that the existing form of what we call ballet, in which dance itself is still only a part of the whole, does not represent the ultimate in choreographic development beyond which no further development is conceivable. Ballet is a form of choreography based on a combination of theatrical devices: props, decor, costume, and lighting. As a result, there is a tendency to dismiss ballet as an "impure" art form, necessarily reliant on theatrical effects by virtue of the fact that it is essentially narrative. But, if it is true that ballet as a form of choreographic art is regarded unfavorably, I have yet to hear any serious objections to choreography itself. I am therefore of the opinion that it is now vital to create alongside the old form a new form of choreographic art in which dance is liberated and self-contained. By confining itself within the narrow limits of narrative-theatrical ballet, the art of dance denies itself the opportunity to show itself in all its glory and provide the supreme choreographic experience.

On occasion—albeit rarely—choreography has been criticized on the grounds that, even if it is not totally reliant on theatrical devices, it cannot exist without music, for in the absence of music it becomes, as it were, a dead art. Attacks of this nature cannot be taken seriously. Choreography is an art founded on the union of music and the movements of the human body. Movement and music are linked by a common discipline—rhythm—and thus constitute the two fundamental elements in the art of choreography.

It has already been pointed out that ballet, given its narrative character, cannot entirely dispense with theatrical devices. However, I would argue that in recent times the theatrical element has begun to take too great a precedence over choreography per se, to the point where the true purpose of the latter has become obscure. It often seems that in the performance of a ballet, the choreography plays the least significant role. Even in more desirable circumstances, where the ballet master is exceptionally inspired, the choreography still fails to dominate the theatrical aspects of the performance. The obvious conclusion is that the existing form of balletic performance does not exploit all available possibilities and that it is up to the defenders of choreography to seek a new choreographic form in which dance is self-sufficient.

I have already stated that ballet as we know it should be retained as one choreographic form among others: there are some excellent ideas in existence that have not as yet been utilized but that can easily be conveyed from the stage by means of the old-style narrative ballet. However, at the same time, there are some splendid themes of fundamental significance that are not contained in any narrative but that could be conveyed directly by means of choreography. (Here, of course, I refer to choreography in its new form.) In the process of creating a new choreographic art form based on dance that is self-contained, it is necessary to strip away all those arts that pertain to the stage and to ruthlessly reject everything that obscures the choreography itself.

In my article on Isadora Duncan, I described the art of dance as a hymn to the imaginary, an anthem to the joy of release, the embodiment of a striving away from the earth toward fantastic heights.[1] Are the stage setting and effects really of such vital importance to the choreographic expression of all of the above? No. It is dance itself that plays the active role, without any need for setting and effects. The art of dance is a great art by virtue of the fact that it is capable of conveying real experiences through movement, but its effects are emotional, rather than visual. Are realistic stage costumes essential to dance? No. All that is essential to dance is a costume that is suitable for dancing. Are stage effects such as thunder, lightning, and wind necessary? No. The art of dance uses movement to recreate all these phenomena for the audience in a more vivid and striking way. Is stage lighting required for dance? Lighting as a facilitating factor, like the frame for a picture, that is maintained at the same level onstage and in the auditorium and changes color at appropriate points is desirable for dance but not indispensable; dance performances in the open air, for example, are perfectly acceptable. Does dance need an orchestra? I have already stated that dance and music are intimately linked; since the orchestra is the most eloquent means of musical expression, it is of course desirable, but the force of what a dance conveys is not diminished if it is performed to a piano accompaniment. Thus, dance—divine movement—together with music—divine language—together constitute the new choreographic art form, which I have termed the dance symphony.

The main principles of this form are as follows:

1. The dance symphony is a choreographic work in several sections executed by any number of performers.
2. The dance symphony is based not on narrative but on an idea that is developed gradually as the sections of the work unfold.
3. Each ballet master has total freedom to order the sections as he wishes.
4. The dance symphony cannot be subdivided into character dances and classical dances but contains both of these as appropriate.

Apart from its main sections, the dance symphony also has an introduction and a conclusion.

The introduction is the point of entry: it prepares the way and hints at what is to follow. The conclusion is a full stop at the end of the performance; it reemphasizes the central idea. The introduction must be linked with the first section and the conclusion with the last.

Plan for a dance symphony on the theme "The Magnificence of the Universe":

Introduction
Section 1: Thermal Energy[a]
Section 2: The Joy of Existence
Section 3: Perpetual Motion
Section 4: Life in Death and Death in Life
Conclusion

The order of the sections may be changed.

In order to show how the theme of "The Magnificence of the Universe" may be treated choreographically, I shall examine each section in turn. (See silhouette drawings 1–20.)

INTRODUCTION AND CONCLUSION

"The Magnificence of the Universe" is the general theme of the proposed dance symphony. As I have indicated earlier, the introduction has a preparatory function while the conclusion completes the work. The first concept in the title of the work is "magnificence." Clearly, the introduction must be devoted exclusively to this concept. The second concept in the title, "the universe," will be the focal point of the conclusion. The intervening sections will illuminate the full meaning of "The Magnificence of the Universe."

Once the ballet master has selected a theme for his dance symphony, he must first of all construct the introduction and the conclusion, for it is in these parts of the work that the theme is stated. It goes without saying that the introduction must be dynamic in character; otherwise, it will not fulfill the function implicit in the term "introduction," that is to say, it will not "lead in" to the work (Latin: intro—inward; ducere— lead). The conclusion, on the other hand, will be static, again because that is what the term "conclusion" implies (Latin: [con]claudere—to shut).

a. The minimal temperature present at the beginning of life.

Figure 1. "The Creation of Light," part 1, "Introduction"

Figure 2. "The Creation of the Sun," part 1, "Introduction"

Figure 3. "The Creation of a Life Source in the Death of a Previous Life," part 2, "Life in Death and Death in Life"

Figure 4. "The Blossoming of Life in Death," part 2, "Life in Death and Death in Life"

Figure 5. "The Creation of a New Life Source," part 2, "Life in Death and Death in Life"

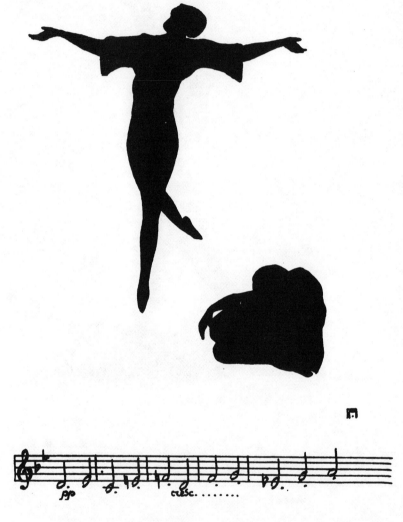

Figure 6. "The Life of a New Life Source," part 2, "Life in Death and Death in Life"

Figure 7. "The Active Pulsating Male Source," part 3, "Thermal Energy"

Figure 8. "The Passive Development of the Female Source," part 3, "Thermal Energy"

Figure 9. "The Active Pulsating Male Source," part 3, "Thermal Energy"

Figure 10. "The Passive Development of the Female Source," part 3, "Thermal Energy"

Figure 11. "The Playfulness of Pithecanthropos," part 4, "The Joy of Existence"

Figure 12. "The Games of the Butterflies," part 4, "The Joy of Existence"

Figure 13. "The Grass Cutters," part 4, "The Joy of Existence"

Figure 14. "The First Flight of the Little Bird," part 4, "The Joy of Existence"

Figure 15. "The Women Going Home from Work," part 4, "The Joy of Existence"

Figure 16. "The Skillful Flight of the Bird," part 4, "The Joy of Existence"

Figure 17. "The Unification of All That Exists through the Joy of Existence," part 4, "The Joy of Existence"

Figure 18. "Perpetual Motion," part 5, "Perpetual Motion"

Figure 19. "Perpetual Motion," part 5, "Perpetual Motion"

Figure 20. "The Universe," part 5, "Perpetual Motion"

To summarize: the introduction to "The Magnificence of the Universe," which is built around the concept of "magnificence," should convey the impression of a stately, solemn procession; the conclusion, which focuses on the idea of "the universe," should be characterized by the same stateliness and solemnity as the introduction, but the manner of its execution should be static.

THERMAL ENERGY

From the choreographic point of view, Thermal Energy consists of dance movements that are calm, even, and separate, not sudden or abrupt. They develop slowly and insinuate themselves into the mind of the spectator like velvet tentacles. They do not burn like fire. The heat flows powerfully, surely, and steadily. This is, of course, a choreographic adagio, but not an adagio of the sort we have seen recently, consisting of intricate flourishes that belong more properly in a circus and bearing little resemblance to an adagio in the true meaning of the word. (I do not object to the occasional eccentric movement if at some point the music demands it, but, nowadays, whether or not the music justifies it, the danseur invariably turns his partner upside down for no other reason than that such acrobatics please the upper-crust audience. For me, an adagio in which the danseur conducts himself like an athlete is not a real adagio.) In a newspaper article, Akim Volynsky remarked that a full downward plié with the subsequent extension of the leg to one side made him think of natural growth stimulated by spring sunshine.[2] This is exactly the impression that must be created by the Thermal Energy adagio. It must possess an insinuating quality and an internal balance. Nothing is static, not even for the briefest moment. In sum, the Thermal Energy adagio consists of slowly unfolding choreographic movements.

PERPETUAL MOTION

Perpetual Motion is related to Thermal Energy in terms of its dynamics, but it is faster and more boisterous. There is more life in it, as it were. Here again nothing is remotely static. No position should be complete, if being complete implies being brought to a standstill. This is an allegro, but an allegro with no sudden movements—steady, regular, operating as if mechanically. Whereas Thermal Energy is contemplative and appeals to the senses, Perpetual Motion involves the spectator in the motion of the dance.

THE JOY OF EXISTENCE

The life of every being is a moment in eternity during which that being has the opportunity to become aware that it is an integral part of the whole of existence. Hence the joy of existence, which is the sensed, intuited realization that the sum of all lives is the universe. The joy of existence is not peculiar to man alone; it is characteristic of every living thing. Let me give some examples: the morning and evening flights of birds, when they soar high into the sky not for the purpose of gathering food but seemingly to sing a hymn to the universe; the games of butterflies in the sunshine; animals gamboling; men and women dancing—all of these are manifestations of the joy of existence.

The choreographic approach is as follows:

1. All four elements of the theme must be coordinated within the dance, for without heat, movement, death, and life the joy of existence is inconceivable.
2. It is necessary to convey through the dance movements all the different ways in which different living things manifest joy, that is to say, to provide a choreographic illustration of folk dancing, flying, crawling, leaping, and so on, all through the prism of joy.

As for the relationship between the static and dynamic movement, it is the latter that dominates. Only the concluding moments of a particular dance section may be static.

LIFE IN DEATH AND DEATH IN LIFE

At first glance, it would appear almost impossible to realize this part choreographically. However, if we bear in mind the fact that the phrase "Life in Death and Death in Life" is built around two concepts, "life" and "death," and that the first is essentially dynamic, while the second is static, the choreographic approach becomes clear. It is quite obvious that, as the title of this section has been broken down into two completely different concepts, the choreography must be based upon two completely different modes of expression—dynamic and static. It can be established that in this part of the work, the dynamic and static elements come together and (more important) concord with each other. It is easy to discover this harmony if we pay attention to the structure of our title. The first part of it, "Life in Death," is dynamic within that which is static, while the second, "Death in Life," is static within that which is dynamic.

The difficulty for the ballet master consists in the problem of how best to combine such different elements: first, *where* should the dynamic begin? and second, *how* to begin the dynamic within the static? Clearly, one individual cannot express these two modes; it is therefore necessary to involve a greater number of participants than in the first two sections, and, indeed, that is what I would advocate. (I stated at the beginning of this chapter that the dance symphony can be executed by any number of performers.) Life in Death is the creation of a new life through death and of many lives through many deaths. Death in Life is the predetermined end of life, since it was from death that life came in the first place. In order to convey all of this choreographically, it is necessary to alternate dynamic and static modes. We must show the creation of a multiplicity of short lives that are then cut short by death (static). But, in that death (static), there should be no sense of finality; rather, there should be a sense of new life being generated. A life in relation to eternity is very short, so the movements depicting it must be short and rapid. They are much faster than those in the Perpetual Motion section, which relate not to a single life but to all of eternity.

Through this analysis, I have endeavored to show that it is indeed possible to approach a theme as difficult as "The Magnificence of the Universe" and to realize it by purely choreographic means. I believe that choreography can achieve much more by proceeding along these lines than it can within the confines of the narrative ballet. I have not yet touched upon the matter of the music for the form of choreography I have described. Ideally, of course, the music should be written specially; this new form would undoubtedly be more attractive to composers than conventional ballet, since it would allow them much greater freedom; they would not be constrained by a story line and all the consequences but would work simply on the basis of the theme and its various sections. However, if the music were not to be specially written, I am sure that it would be much easier to find suitable music for this form than for narrative ballet. Indeed, it might not be necessary to look very hard at all; there are many suitable pieces of music already in existence.

Dance Symphonism

Very frequently, especially in recent times, the view has been expressed that the next natural stage in the development of dance is its "symphonization."[1] But how to "symphonize" dance? No one is able to answer this question, least of all those who talk about it the most. There has been some attempt to make dance more "symphonic" over the past five to seven years to the extent that dance productions have been created to the music of symphonic poems.[2] This is a welcome step for two reasons. First, it marks a final release from the archaic music of a dead era and the start of a new age in which choreography will be given the meaningful musical accompaniment it deserves. Second, we are well acquainted with symphonic music, and that familiarity makes it easier for us to see how to progress toward the symphonization of dance—a desirable end, for, while purely symphonic music is the pinnacle of music as art, dance has yet to scale an equivalent height. However, it would be absurd to make claims about the symphonic nature of dance simply on the grounds that it is set to symphonic music, if it does not itself possess any of the characteristics of symphonism. How, then, can symphonism in a dance work—be it a single variation, a whole act, a ballet, or a dance symphony—be achieved? Only by basing the staging of any dance—from minor variations to full-scale ballets, not to mention dance symphonies—on the principle of thematic choreographic development,[3] instead of on a random selection of dance movements, even if they are performed in time to the music. The principle of thematic choreographic development is the very essence of dance symphonism, whether the dance work being staged is small (a variation) or large (a whole ballet).

If we analyze existing works of choreography, both individual numbers and whole ballets, we find that, prior to Fokine, there were no elements of symphonism, in that there were no compositions based on the development of choreographic themes.[4] If there were occasional leanings in this direction, they were entirely fortuitous. Among the thousands of variations known to us, there are several "accidental" manifestations of symphonism: a particularly good example is Raymonda's variation from the last act of the eponymous ballet. The movement on which the variation is based throughout—the pas de bourrée[5] and a character dance motif (whose Russian name means "little rope") performed on pointe—are developed comprehensively. The variation contains only these two types of movement from start to finish; hence its captivating charm and gravity. I am not arguing that every variation must be restricted to the use of only one or two dance movements; far from it: there may be one, two, three, or even more movements, but what matters is that they should not be random movements but movements developed in conjunction with one another.

Raymonda's variation is the only one with elements of symphonism carried through to the end without a change of tone. There are other variations in which symphonism is partially present, but the majority are constructed out of a totally random selection of dance movements, none of which is at all elaborated. Among the variations that cannot be taken seriously in choreographic terms is the one from the ballet *Pygmalion*, which in recent years has usually been performed by ballerinas in the "Jardin Animé" scene of the ballet *Le Corsaire*.[6] Here we have any number of steps of a purely exhibitionist nature, as if the dancer were taking a sixty-second examination before the public, repeatedly throwing her legs out in a développé toward the end in order to dazzle the audience with a final piece of brilliance.[7] This entire variation is nothing but a mishmash of unconnected movements thrown together without any justification, a sort of balletic mixed salad. The same may be said of the vast majority of variations.

It is perfectly understandable why the variation from *Raymonda* is never performed at private concerts. The variation is difficult, because, for the duration of a whole minute, a single step—the pas de bourrée, danced on pointe and interwoven with a character motif—is fully developed. The performance must be exceptionally good, because the spectator has plenty of time to observe whether the movement is smooth or blurred; only a very experienced ballerina is capable of dancing the variation successfully.

When we look at whole ballets from the pre-Fokine period, we find among the many works in existence only two that contain dance symphonism, and then only in part. One is the second act of *Giselle;* the other is the fourth act of *Swan Lake,* before the entrance of the sorcerer Rothbart.

Dance symphonism is evident in two-thirds of the second act of *Giselle.* Four dance motifs are elaborated in the course of the act: a port de bras, arabesque, saut de basque, and jeté.[8] These four motifs are developed for two-thirds of the act but unfortunately are diluted by the interjection of random movements sharply at variance with them. The Wilis, who are impassive, perform a dance based on impassive movements. The port de bras is about reaching out; the arabesque signifies soaring, the saut de basque is about motion and the jeté striving: none of these movements reveals any trace of earthly passion if they are performed in accordance with the principles of classical dance, without any emotional overtones or contemporary touches. The result is precisely what is required for the second act of *Giselle.* At the same time, it is vexing to see movements inserted that are inappropriate for the Wilis and, moreover, of very short duration and completely undeveloped. These intrusive elements are evidence of the fact that the second act of *Giselle* was not constructed on the basis of thematic choreographic development but put together from randomly selected dance movements; the dance symphonism we observe can only be the result of the intuitive talent of Petipa.

There is a far more significant example of symphonism in Act IV of *Swan Lake* before Rothbart's entrance. I consider this act—staged by Petipa and Ivanov jointly—the most accomplished of their choreographic works.[9] It does not contain any random or undeveloped dance movements. The main motif of this act—the grieving swans' arm motif with the leg in battement tendu—is developed in all positions by the whole ensemble. I am one of the few who regard this act as the height of choreographic perfection in that it consistently embodies the principle of thematic development. At the beginning of this chapter, I stated that such an approach was unknown among choreographers, yet this act forces me to reconsider: perhaps the prize for first place in dance symphonism should be awarded after all to Ivanov and Petipa. On the other hand, the second act of *Swan Lake*, which is usually so highly praised, suffers from serious defects from the point of view of dance symphonism.

With Fokine, dance symphonism becomes conspicuous in ballet productions, not in his early works but subsequently—in *Les Préludes*, to the music of Liszt, in the opera *Orfeo*, to the music of Gluck (notably the scenes of hell and paradise), in the *Polovtsian Dances*, to the music of Borodin: in these works the dances are based upon a thematic choreographic development that is strictly adhered to, without the addition of a single random movement.[10] Some may ask whether this approach is really necessary, for might not the whole fascination of dance lie precisely in the randomness of its movements? We can obtain a clear answer to this question by asking even someone unschooled in choreography which ballets are the most pleasing. The answer is always the same—*Giselle, Swan Lake, The Sleeping Beauty, Polovtsian Dances,* and *Chopiniana*—in other words, those very ballets in which, on closer analysis, we discover the presence of thematic choreographic development or the counteraction, conflict, and conjunction of choreographic themes.[11] By contrast, those ballets in which the whole composition is made up of random movements are generally regarded as the least distinguished from the artistic point of view. What better indication could there be of the path the art of choreography should follow?

To summarize: the staging of a dance may be nonsymphonic, regardless of the fact that it is performed to the accompaniment of symphonic music, if it is based upon randomly selected and carelessly distributed dance movements. Conversely, a choreographic work may be fully symphonic even when it is performed to the accompaniment of nonsymphonic music, though in this case there is, of course, a serious mismatch between the choreographic and the musical intentions.

The ideal form of choreographic creativity involves close contact between musical and dance symphonism.

The Position of Dance in Relation to Music: Separate, Dominant, Subordinate, and Integrated

According to what we hear or read on posters advertising ballet or opera productions, dances are performed "to the accompaniment of music" or are "set" to music. We may well conclude from these phrases that, for the most part, the dance and the music are not integrated. The idea of treating dance and music as one is very new: it was first put forward less than five years ago.[1] It cannot be attributed to any particular choreographer or musician; rather, it evolved spontaneously and began to take root in the world of dance criticism because it provided the most accurate description of a phenomenon of which we were already instinctively aware. However, no one has yet succeeded in demonstrating why it is that a particular dance production achieves an integration of dance and music, whereas another does not (although examples of the former, it must be said, are very rare).

Musicians have made only limited efforts in this direction; they have gone no further than determining the rhythm of a dance and ensuring that it coincides more or less with the rhythm of the music. To date, all discussions of the possibility of basing dance productions on the integration of dance and music are merely the expression of a wish based on instinct and the realization that mistakes have been made in the past. Neither musicians nor choreographers have been able to come up with any concrete suggestions as to what the integration of dance and music might actually mean in real terms, because neither the musician nor the choreographer is fully acquainted with both arts: however considerable his expertise, each is confined to his own area of specialization. Yet, until dance and music—two arts that are so close to one another, "whose fore-fathers, sound and gesture, were born together"—are recognized as one, discussions about the possibility of integrating dance and music will lead nowhere.

Before I proceed, I feel I must mention the all too obvious contempt with which musicians (with a few rare exceptions) regard choreography. One might expect that musicians, of all people, would take the trouble to understand the power of our art, instead of looking down upon it condescendingly and arguing against the use of certain musical pieces for choreographic purposes on the grounds that such use would not be appropriate. Musicians are making the same mistake in relation to choreography that choreography (in the person of the ballet master) once made in relation to music—a subject to which I shall return later. There is NO music that is 100 percent suitable for choreography. What is important in a dance production is that the choreography and the music should not be at odds with each other. It is high time that we abandoned the idea of specially simplified music that is "danceable," to use a loathsome expression. I am not opposed to the use of "danceable" music for ballet, the old form of choreographic art, but it should not be forgotten that ballet is not the limit of choreographic achievement: we have now progressed to a new form—the dance symphony or symphonism in dance—which obviates the need for special dance music.

In short, to stage productions based upon the integration of dance and music, a knowledge of both dance and music is essential. We should not wait until musicians, with their scornful or at best indulgent attitude, deign to study choreography so as to be able to provide choreographers with the assistance they need. Instead, we as choreographers must take up the study of music and thereby free ourselves from the many contradictions by which we are currently beset. This alternative provides a faster and more convenient solution to the current problem, because choreographers would need far less time to learn about music than musicians would need to learn about choreography. The fact is that the basics of music are available to every educated individual for the simple reason that music is all around us and is easily accessible, but the same cannot be said of choreography, which is very specialized and has not yet gained universal acceptance. If we compare the levels of knowledge of music and choreography found among practitioners of each of the two arts, it immediately becomes obvious that, whereas musicians know virtually nothing about choreography, choreographers have at least some knowledge of music. Of course, one must not generalize, but I think that we have here a clear enough indication of the direction from which we might expect practical steps to be taken toward the unification of music and dance.

The integration of dance and music implies a fusion of gesture and sound, not just at the obvious level of rhythm (corresponding beats) but also on another level, to which I shall return later. However, before I discuss the principles that underlie the integration of dance and music, I shall first of all examine three other types of relationship between dance and music, which I shall refer to as "dance with music" (where the dance and the music are virtually unconnected), "dance to the accompaniment of music" (where music plays a secondary role), and "dance set to music" (where music plays the dominant role).

Before the concept of integration of dance and music emerged, there existed (and still exists) another notion: that of dance as being either rhythmic or nonrhythmic. I do not consider these terms adequate, for the rhythmicity of a dance cannot be defined simply in terms of its superficial synchronization with the beat of the music. Obviously, "rhythm" has become confused with "meter." Every dance, regardless of the kind of music to which it is performed, must match the music in terms of its measure, by which I mean that it must be similarly divided up into beats: if the measures are different, the two sets of beats will conflict with each other. If the visible measure of the dance does not coincide with the audible measure of the music, the lack of correspondence jars. At some point in the distant past, this sense of mismatch became confused with the concept of rhythm, and out of the confusion there developed the notion that dance itself was either rhythmic or nonrhythmic. Thus, for a dance to be considered rhythmic, its movements would have to be fitted into a measure that corresponded to the measure of the music—three beats to a bar, or whatever.

Let me give an example. There are four parts to the simple dance movement of the polka:

1. beginning with the left foot, take one step forward;
2. bring the right foot up to join the left foot;
3. with the left foot take a step in place;
4. hop on the left foot while lifting the right foot in the air.

If a quaver is allocated to each of these four movements, they will all fit into one bar in $\frac{2}{4}$ time (see music example 6). But these four movements would not fit into a three-beat bar, given that each movement is of a quaver's duration. The fourth movement of the polka would lose its musical place (see music example 7). Of course, it could be moved into the following bar, but dance that is divided into bars has strong beats and weak beats, just as music does.[2] Every dance (including the polka, which is a rather trivial example) has strong and weak beats, and any attempt to set the weak beat of a dance movement against a strong musical beat will evoke in an audience not a sense of harmony but—to use the old terminology—a suspicion that the dance has been staged "unrhythmically." It might be possible to increase or decrease the duration of the

Пример № 2а   Пример № 2б

Music examples 6 and 7

individual movement from a quaver to a crotchet or a semi-quaver without altering the time of the dance step as a whole, were it not for the fact that the strong and the weak beats of the dance must coincide with those of the music.

All stage dance productions up to the time of the first attempts to integrate dance and music have been based without exception upon the principle of bar-by-bar correspondence, for stage dance developed out of folk dance, which, being indifferent to the essential character of the music that accompanied it, was itself based upon this principle.[3] All stage dance productions, past and present, are characterized by an apparent rhythmicity: that is to say, the dance seems to go together with the music. It is true that both choreographers and musicians have more and more frequently been heard to complain that these productions are "not properly integrated," but no one has as yet managed to offer any evidence in support of this claim or to suggest a solution to the problem.

"Dance to the accompaniment of music," "dance set to music," and the integration of dance with music to which we currently aspire—three kinds of relationship between dance and music—seem at first glance to be virtually indistinguishable from each other, but first glances are deceptive. On closer examination, the differences among these three relationships become blindingly obvious (the actual words used in their descriptions provide an indication of where the dissimilarities lie). The practice of staging dance "to the accompaniment of music" belongs to the past; nowadays this practice is considered incorrect, and only those who are ill informed in matters of choreography continue to turn to it. The idea of "setting dance to music" dominates in the modern age. The integration of dance and music is the choreography of the future, a future that is already upon us.

Before the age of "dance to the accompaniment of music," there was an earlier age of "dance with music." Dance is at an earlier stage of development than music.[a] At a time when

a. For this analysis I shall be referring only to choreographic works for the theater.

the art of choreography was starting to take shape in theatrical terms and was developing the beginnings of a form—ballet— the art of music already possessed clear forms. Theatrical dance, being linked to music, was forced into an association with it that was closer than the association that existed between folk dance and its musical accompaniment. Theatrical dance, in fact, was forced to make a real effort, using all the means available to it, to become united with music.

The initial link between dance and music, which I have described as "dance with music," is characterized by a total lack of correspondence between the two, even on the level of rhythm.[4] In those far-off times, it was acceptable to stage a two-beat dance to three-beat music. The age of "dance to the accompaniment of music," which followed the age of "dance with music," suffered the effects of these archaic errors, and the effects are still in evidence today. The ballet master Marius Petipa, whom I associate with the age of dance to the accompaniment of music, tolerated precisely this sort of lack of correspondence in his ballet productions. In *Swan Lake,* the three-beat coda in Act I accompanies dances in two beats.[5] The Saracen dance in Act II of *Raymonda,* the music of which has three beats, has dance movements of two beats. These are only the most obvious examples. There are countless more minor errors in the ballets of the past. These errors, which we find in the age of dance to the accompaniment of music, are proof of the existence of the initial "dance with music" stage that I have postulated, when dance movements were set to music for theatrical performance in such a way that there was no correspondence between dance and music, even in terms of measure.

In subsequent phases in the development of the art of dance, ballet masters and dance directors, confronted with music that was more sophisticated than the dance, were obliged to take note of and to try to correct the errors of their predecessors. Dance with music, dance to the accompaniment of music, and dance set to music are steps—each an improvement on the one before—along the road leading to a closer unity with music and the elaboration of a single true principle: the integration of dance and music. The leaders of the world of dance looked at music from all sides, as it were, before finally realizing that the only way to create harmony between music and dance is to unite the two into a single whole.

To summarize: the first stage in the development of theatrical dance is "dance with music," which tolerates a complete lack of correspondence between the measure of the dance movements and that of the accompanying music. Dance and music go their separate ways. They are completely unrelated to each other both in general terms and in all essential details: harmony, tonality, intensity, and tempo. Under these circumstances there can be no question of rhythmic correspondence, even bar-to-bar correspondence. The remnants of this archaic stage of theatrical dance—dance with music—can still be seen today in circus fantasias, dances based on fairy-tale themes and performed as circus acts. These dances are devised and performed with complete disregard for the music that accompanies them. The directors are not concerned with measure and harmony or the appropriateness of the music to the mood of the piece. They do not ask themselves whether the feelings of melancholy evoked by events on stage at a particular point will be enhanced by the major tonality that happens to announce itself in the music at that same moment,[6] or whether the music is suitable for an onstage andante or allegro; these and a number of other more subtle questions never arise. The surviving circus fantasias have become fossilized in the early stage of the development of dance—"dance with music"—and all of the concerns I have mentioned are irrelevant to them. The music is one distinct aspect of a performance, the action is another.

Regrettably, the mime scenes in the ballets created by ballet masters up to and including Petipa are not so very different from circus fantasias. Not a single one of Petipa's ballets has mime scenes that correspond to the music. Not a single gesture is linked to the music through measure, rhythm, or mood. Artists may execute the movements however they choose, with complete disregard for the music; one will achieve good results, another bad, depending on the individual's level of talent. What we see here is nothing other than mime-improvisation. The ballet master composing a mime mise-en-scène did not stop to ask himself whether it was appropriate, given the music at a particular point, for the dancer to act out such-and-such a mood. All the works by ballet masters up to and including Petipa suffer from this archaic approach. I do not intend to dwell upon individual examples, but as a diversion I will describe the comical final mime scene from the ballet *The Daughter of Pharaoh*,[7] in which Aspicia, on her knees before Pharaoh, begs him to pardon Ta-Hor, who has been sentenced to death by snakebite. This scene would inspire terror were it not accompanied by a modern bravura march with almost comical bass drumbeats of the sort that accompany the death of a clown in the circus. It could be argued in Petipa's defense that the music for this ballet was written almost in its entirety with the principle of "dance with music" in mind. However, Petipa cannot be forgiven for approaching the music of Tchaikovsky and Glazunov in the same way. In the works of these composers, every nuance of theme and story line is elaborated in musical terms both in the pure dance and in the mime sections, and everything is so perfectly clearcut that, with a little understanding, it should be possible to achieve perfect harmony between the music and the choreographic action on stage.[8]

After the period of dance "with music," the next stage in the development of choreography in terms of the relationship between dance and music was the stage of "dance to the accompaniment of music." (I will omit the transitional period in which the two stages coexisted as a result of the fact that the new principles were being introduced at a time when the old ones were still in place.) Dance "to the accompaniment of music" is far more sophisticated than dance "with music." It is closer to the music in the way that a rider is close to his horse, urging it on in whatever direction he pleases (though, even when choreography had succeeded in harnessing music with a view to subjugating it completely, ballet masters still found that they were forced in spite of themselves to respond to the demands made by the music). Ballet masters realized that dance productions created on the basis of the "dance with music" principle were not successful. Choreography was striving to come alive, but, in order to do so, it had to improve. Such improvement could come about only through a more careful treatment of accompanying music. Music in this period really was only an accompaniment; it was not considered a force to be reckoned with. Yet, at the same time, the wish to heighten the impact of dance brought dance and music closer together: in staging dance productions, efforts were made to select music that might not have always been entirely appropriate but that at least reflected the mood of the dance to some extent. If the action required a minor key, a minor key was provided, albeit to order and without too much concern for the finer details.

In the sphere of pure dance, rhythmicity began to assume importance, as can be seen from the correspondence between the musical and the dance measures and from the fact that significant moments in the music and the dance coincided. Strong and weak beats in the dance were identified and then allocated to musical beats of similar quality. However, this was done within the space of a single bar; all subsequent bars were made to follow suit until the musical measure changed or a new melody began. Ballet masters of the time failed to understand that melody in a consistent meter is homogeneous only in that the bars unerringly follow one another. Bars of the same measure are similar to the extent that they have the same number of weak and strong beats, but that is where the similarity ends. Bars that are genuinely identical in every respect are found only in the course of thematic development; there may even be very many of them, but their repeated occurrences are embedded in the structure of the musical composition as a whole. (Note that I refer here only to similar bars in the same key; bars that are similar but in different keys I do not consider identical because each key has its own distinctive color.)[9] Nothing is known of the way in which dance approached extended works with numerous rhythmic variations in the period of "dance to the accompaniment of music," nor do we know anything of the thematic development of dance, although there was certainly thematic development in the ballet music of that time, which should have prompted ballet masters to seek a choreographic equivalent. A sort of harmony between dance and music was established, but it was monotonous, for the supposed match between the rhythm of the dance work and the accompanying music amounted to nothing more than an approximate correspondence within the space of a single bar that was then reproduced over a whole number of subsequent bars.

By way of example, I shall consider the organization of the dance of the Wilis from the second act of *Giselle* (see music example 8).[10] The dance performed to the accompaniment of this music is relatively rhythmic; that is to say, it reflects the homogeneity of the bars in that it follows a single pattern over seven bars, ♪♫♫ ♪♫♫ with emphasis on the first and fourth quavers. However, when we look for a correspondence

Music example 8. All the dance movements listed here are more or less turns that maintain the effect of one level. The renversé curve moves upward because, although the renversé is a turn, it nevertheless has the character of a movement that moves forward and upward as a result of the fact that the leg is raised. The pas de bourrée is circular, so the curve describes a circle. The arabesque croisée moves backward, and consequently the curve descends. The chaîné is an energetic forward movement, for which the graphic equivalent is an upward curve.

between the movement of the melody and the movements of
the dance, we find instead a sharp divergence (compare the
curve of the melody with that of the dance movements). The
melody, all bars of which apparently follow a similar pattern,
steadily strives upward and then abruptly descends within the
space of one bar, as can be seen from the curved melody line
(drawn on a staff beneath the musical notes for the purpose of
illustration). But the curve of the dance (also drawn on a staff)
does not move in the same way. The dance curve is distinctly
steady, because the dance movements in this section are steady,
consisting as they do of turns that do not travel. The pas de
bourrée en tournant, both en dedans and en dehors, and the
renversé all fall into this category of steady movements, and so
does the arabesque in this section, first, because it is framed on
either side by a pas de bourrée en tournant, and, second, because
it is croisé, which makes it less recognizably an arabesque. (A
true arabesque is effacé and of longer duration than the quaver
that is allocated to it here.) Only in the second half of the
seventh bar does the movement of the dance turn upward.

I am not concerned here with the composition of the individual dance movements, since they fall within the bar rhythm
in the section in question. What concerns me is the overall
mismatch between this particular section of the dance and its
corresponding melody. In the music, there is a striving upward,
a relentless intensification with temporary relapses; the effect is
comparable to the movement of waves breaking on the shore.
In the dance, on the other hand, we find the dogged repetition
of an on-the-spot turn with an uncertain movement upward
in the eighth bar, when in fact, judging by the movement of
the melody, there should have been a descent. If we look at
these eight bars as they are written, or indeed if we simply listen to the melody, it is immediately obvious that it is suggestive
of repetition and stability: ♩♫♫♫ ♩♫♫♫ However, we also
need to look at the sum of the parts the music comprises.
The listener's first impression is that these eight bars are all similar to one another. The first six are actually almost identical.
And yet, at the same time, they are different, in the way that

twins are different in their character and internal makeup, even though externally they are alike.

In staging the dance, the music has been divided into equal segments consisting of two bars each, an approach typical of ballet masters of the period of "dance to the accompaniment of music." The ballet master chose to disregard the fact that, every two bars, the melody turns upward. Having taken the first two bars as his model and being under the impression that the remaining bars were more of the same, since they were all based on the same pattern ♪♫♫♫ ♪♫♫♫ he set four dance movements to the first two bars and then simply repeated them for each subsequent pair of bars, finishing with a typical classical dance ending—chaîné turns down the diagonal—in bars 7 and 8. Personally, I have always found the chaîné turn irritating because, although it is an amazing, highly expressive dance movement, it has always been used as a last resort where the complexity of the movement of the music has made it difficult to find an appropriate dance equivalent. Variations, codas, entrances—all end with chaînés, even when the music does not even hint at energetic, vortical movement."[11] Card players have a saying: "If you have nothing to lead with, play a diamond." Ballet masters of the past took a similar line: if they lacked the imagination to bring a section of dance to a suitable close, they simply fell back on chaînés.

In the period of "dance to the accompaniment of music," the principle behind the staging of individual dances was always the same. It can be formulated as follows: the first step was to look at the musical work in order to identify the phrases[12] into which it would be crudely divided for the purposes of staging the dance. The usual form of the work was "beginning-middle-end": music was written to the specifications of the ballet master, who usually demanded that the form should be thus. (All ballet variations up to the time of Alexander Gorsky and Fokine provide clear evidence that this was the case. On rare occasions, we find an addition to the three-part form described: an accelerated finale for chaînés or jetés en tournant—never mind that such energetic turns may not have been in keeping with the action onstage or the mood of the variation.) Dance movements were then set to the opening bars of the phrases that had been identified, and those same movements were repeated over and over again until the melody came to an end.[13]

A good example of this approach is Albrecht's variation from the second act of *Giselle*.[14] I have selected this piece not because it provides exceptional support for my case but because I happen to have the score of the variation at hand. Any other variation would serve equally well to illustrate the point that all variations of the period of "dance to the accompaniment of music" were alike in being constructed in the way I have described. The two bars of the introduction to this variation (see music example 9) are not accompanied by any dance movements. Although, in this particular case, movements may not be necessary, it cannot be regarded as a rule that introductions should be devoid of movement, because some introductions are very long. However, in the age of "dance to the accompaniment of music," introductions, cadences, and modulations were always devoid of dance movements.[15] The introduction is sometimes extensive, acting as a sort of threshold to the melody that follows; the same is true of the modulation that occurs in the middle of a variation. But both the introduction and the modulation are difficult in the sense that they do not obviously contain a phrase (rhythmic unit) or melody (melodic unit) that is easily remembered by the listener; consequently, they are always ignored, and the dancer must wait for the start of the phrase, either standing still or lurking in the wings, from which he makes his

Пример № 4

Music example 9

entrance at the very last moment. If the introduction is very long, the danseur or danseuse executes an "empty" run across the stage to the position from which he or she must begin the variation. The ballet master of the age of "dance to the accompaniment of music" did not take account of the fact that by no means every long introduction indicates walking or running.

The first eight bars of Albrecht's variation constitute the first of the three sections of the variation:[16] they make up the beginning and contain a phrase (rhythmic unit) and melody to which the ballet master sets dance movements (see music example 10). The ballet master notes that the phrase can be broken down without difficulty into sixteen beats, with two beats to the bar. These sixteen beats can easily be further broken down into 2, 4, and 8. He also notes that the melody (melodic unit), which encompasses sixteen beats, can also be broken down into 2, 4, and 8, with each part that results from the division

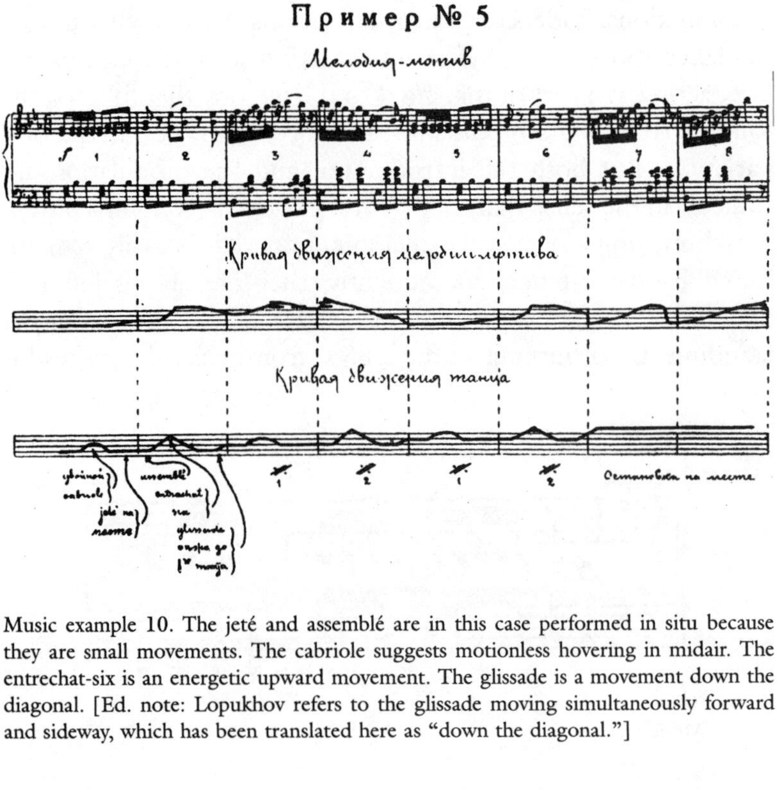

Music example 10. The jeté and assemblé are in this case performed in situ because they are small movements. The cabriole suggests motionless hovering in midair. The entrechat-six is an energetic upward movement. The glissade is a movement down the diagonal. [Ed. note: Lopukhov refers to the glissade moving simultaneously forward and sideway, which has been translated here as "down the diagonal."]

containing an element of the melody as a whole. In the present case, the sixteen-beat melody was divided into four equal parts, each containing two bars. For the ballet master of the age of "dance to the accompaniment of music," that was quite sufficient. He divided the whole of the first part of the variation into apparently equal parts of two bars each. The fact that the third and fourth bars were quite unlike the first two in terms of musical structure and movement was of no concern to him. Having arranged the dance movements as I have indicated (under the curve of the movement of the dance in music example 10), the ballet master realized that these same movements would also fit exactly into the next two bars of the melody. It did not matter to him that the double cabriole, which was a brilliant match for the semiquavers of the first bar, was not at all appropriate for the third bar: whereas the first bar is stable, in the third bar the melody moves upward and proceeds in semiquaver leaps that lend it a sparkling character. He simply saw that the movements he had arranged would continue to fit within the rhythm of the bars, so he repeated the movements from the first two bars three times, stopping at the seventh and eighth bars in order to prepare for the next part of the variation.

This is a typical approach, and it shows how far the center of attention had shifted away from the music to the dance. If we compare the curve of the movement of the music with the curve of the movement of the dance (music example 10), we see that only the first and the fifth bars show any correspondence. The persistent semiquavers of the first and fifth bars, which pause only momentarily, are matched by the double cabriole that stops momentarily in midair. Apart from this, there is no other point of correspondence in the whole of the first part of the variation. Elsewhere, the curves diverge: where the music descends, the dance rises, and vice versa. This is particularly evident where the entrechat-six is performed in bars 2 and 6. The entrechat finishes (that is to say, the dancer touches the ground) precisely at the point where the melody takes a sudden turn upward.[17] Furthermore, while the first two bars can at least be said to achieve a fair degree of harmony between dance and music by virtue of the fact that there are several points of correspondence, the exact repetition of the dance movements from these two bars in the third and fourth bars is totally unacceptable: bars 3 and 4 have a completely new sound, and the movement of the melody is different (toward the end of the fourth bar, it falls back down to its starting point). The dance movements in bars 1 and 2 strive forward undeviatingly; there is no suggestion of forward striving in the music of bars 3 and 4. Therefore, the movements should not be repeated until bars 5 and 6, which are virtually the same as bars 1 and 2. Bars 7 and 8 also suggest forward striving (the melody moves forward and upward), so, of course, the passivity of the dancer in expectation of the second part of the variation is completely out of place.

The same principle underlies the staging of the second part of the variation (see music example 11). In identical fashion, dance movements are devised for the first two bars and then repeated. In the seventh and eighth bars, the dancer runs to the back of the stage. In this instance, the arrangement for the first four bars is acceptable; although not all the details are correct, at least the curve of the melody and the curve of the dance are apparently at one with each other. However, from the fifth bar onward there is complete divergence, for in the fifth bar the melody returns to its starting point (the beginning of the first part of the variation), whereas the dance movements are a repetition of the first and second bars of the second part of the variation. The melody in bars 7 and 8 of the second part is a repetition of the melody in bars 7 and 8 of the first part.

In part three, the double tours en l'air in bars 10 and 12 are undoubtedly good because they reflect the movement of the music brilliantly. Both dance and music strive upward and then fall back down. There are also similarities—though fewer—between dance and music in the ninth and eleventh bars. The thirteenth and fourteenth bars should not contain repeat dance movements because here the melody again returns to the first and second bars of part 1 of the variation. There is again a clear connection in bars 15 and 16 (in spite of the fact that the pirouette is executed on the spot), because the energy of the turning movement matches the energetic upward movement of the music.[18]

This examination of Albrecht's variation in its entirety shows that, in general, harmony and correspondence between music and dance are woefully lacking. (We have not even begun to consider whether the dance movements are good in themselves.) And yet, if we look carefully at the respective curves of the music and the dance, we can see quite clearly that in fact it would be possible, with just a little attention to the music on the part of the ballet master, to achieve total harmony. Both curves follow the same principle of symmetry, but it is differently applied. Differing application of symmetry is a typical feature of

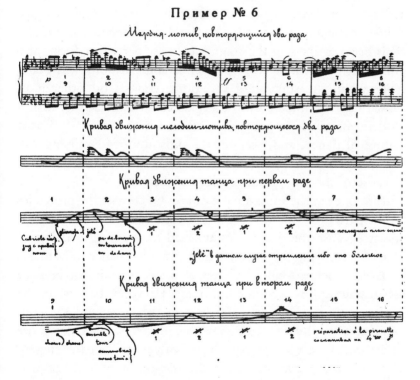

Music example 11. The chassé in this instance is a forward movement. The assemblé is insignificant here as its function is to prepare for the tour en l'air. The tour en l'air is a stronger, more energetic upward movement than the entrechat-six because of the midair turn.

the age of "dance to the accompaniment of music." The choreographers of that period happily ignored the fact that music
possessed a pace, movement, and form of its own. Obviously, if
dance movements are to be arranged to music that has already
been composed, harmony and correspondence will be achieved
only by taking the characteristics of the music into account, not
by simply dividing the music into memorable tunes and more
often than not forgetting about important details.

In the treatment of variations, codas, and other individual
dance numbers from the period of "dance to the accompaniment of music," we see the glimmerings of a desire to integrate
dance and music, although the attempts to do so follow the
pattern I have just described in my analysis of Albrecht's variation. However, in the case of mime and duets, this tendency
is far less evident. In the vast majority of cases, the staging of
mime and duets was still on the level of "dance with music."
This backwardness in the staging of these particular forms at a
time when increased correspondence and harmony was being
achieved in the staging of variations, codas, and other individual dance numbers can be explained by two factors: first, a
disdain for music in general, combined with the self-sufficient
nature of dance, and, second, the difficulty of identifying significant points in the melodies of duets and mime sequences
because of the complicating effect of thematic development—a
feature of even the most simple music. Of course, the principles
of the period of "dance with music" did not survive completely
intact because the practice established for staging variations—
that of identifying the melodies and arranging dance movements
to them—inclined ballet masters to resort to a similar practice
when staging mime scenes and duets. However, because of the
unequal number of parts and bars in the latter and the consequent difficulty of identifying melodies,[19] we find far more
archaisms from the age of "dance with music" in the staging
of these pieces than we find in the staging of episodes of pure
dance.

In 1889, the year Tchaikovsky began to write the music for
ballet,[20] the age of "dance to the accompaniment of music"

gave way to the age of "dance set to music." With this ballet, Tchaikovsky opened up a whole new era for the art of choreography, though, strangely enough, it was not to be an era of progress. One might have expected that, once choreography had been recognized by the greatest of composers, it would scale previously unattainable heights, but, in fact, the opposite happened. In my view, the first ballet from the age of "dance set to music," Tchaikovsky's *The Sleeping Beauty,* is 50 percent less successful in terms of its harmony and correspondence with the music than Nikolai Krotkov's *Les Caprices du Papillon,* which I regard as the last ballet from the age of "dance to the accompaniment of music," although both ballets were staged by Petipa. In general, I would describe the age of "dance set to music," which began with Tchaikovsky and in which we find ourselves at present, as a necessary stage in the progression toward the ideal—the integration of dance and music—but one that is actually unfavorable to choreography. In the age of "dance set to music," choreography is completely subordinated to music. On the positive side, this subordination has led to awareness, and through this awareness the integration of dance and music has become a possibility.

If choreographers in the age of "dance to the accompaniment of music" had paid more attention to the music and had ceased to look down upon it, they would have been better prepared for the more complex resonances contained in the music of Tchaikovsky and his successors. They certainly would not have ended up in the hopeless situation that Petipa, despite his exceptional talent for inventing imaginative dance arrangements, found himself in when he came to stage *The Sleeping Beauty.* Following the first production of *The Sleeping Beauty,* not only did choreography fail to win any new laurels, but it actually lost some of the ground it had gained. This backward slide ceased with the appearance of Fokine, but by then the art of music was making such great strides forward that choreography seemed to fall behind even when it was standing still. A lack of progression is effectively the same as regression. We as choreographers have endless means at our disposal in terms of dance movements, so we must advance and take up the position to which we and our art are entitled. However, there is only one way to do this: to study the constantly developing art of music.

After 1890, then, choreography moved abruptly from the age of "dance to the accompaniment of music" to the age of "dance set to music," without being fully aware of the nature of the change that had taken place. Choreographers, in particular Petipa and Ivanov, who had grown accustomed to dealing with "subordinate" ballet music—music in a long-established form that was easy to manage and posed no problems when it came to staging dance and mime scenes—applied the same tried-and-true methods to Tchaikovsky's *The Sleeping Beauty*. However, if the strategy of identifying a melody and dividing it into equal parts was still just about workable in the time of "dance to the accompaniment of music" (when music was written to order to the extent that it was possible to request the insertion of a certain number of bars "without any emotional content"), it certainly ceased to be so when applied to the music of Tchaikovsky and the ballet composers who followed him. The principles according to which the masters of the new age of "dance set to music" wrote ballet music were completely different from those of the masters of the old age of "dance to the accompaniment of music." In the first place, it would never have occurred to the old-style composers to provide a particular character with a musical theme that would be developed in the course of the ballet.[21] Only in the rarest of cases were characters identified by musical themes; they were hardly ever associated with music that recurred—sometimes in a modified form depending upon the action—throughout the ballet. For example, if at some point there was a mimed argument between two very different characters, the accompanying music would focus on the argument itself and not on the individuals involved; in other words, neither of the characters was conveyed in musical-thematic terms, only the impression of the argument.

Let me cite two examples. The first is the argument between Nikiya and Gamzatti in Act II of *La Bayadère*. The ballet master—and, indeed, any listener—can identify in the musical accompaniment an argument between two jealous women and a melodic allusion to the love scene in the opening act of the ballet. However, there is no hint in the music either of the powerful and angry Gamzatti or of the powerless but loving Nikiya. The second example is the meeting in the fisherman's hut between the Nubian king and Aspicia in *The Daughter of Pharaoh*. This music makes us aware that there is, on the one hand, a person (not necessarily a woman) who is frightened by the appearance of someone unexpected and, on the other, an enamored and impetuous persecutor; it does not show us either Aspicia, the Pharaoh's daughter, or the Nubian king. I will not mention any further examples, for all such mime scenes are the same. Nikiya and Gamzatti could act out their argument dressed in Spanish costumes without in any way weakening the connection between the action and the music, since the music does not tell us anything at all about the characters themselves. Everything I have said could equally well apply to any scene in any ballet from the age of "dance to the accompaniment of music." To restate my point in the simplest possible terms, *La Bayadère* might just as well be performed to the music of *The Daughter of Pharaoh*.

Not only mime scenes were affected in this way but dance scenes, as well. Where, for example, are the musical differences between the variation danced by Aspicia in the Act I hunt scene and Lise's variation in the second act of *La Fille Mal Gardée*?[22] There are none. Neither variation would be out of place in any ballet, and the ballet would not be noticeably different as a result. Indeed, ballerinas often did use variations from other ballets; they do so today in ballets the music for which precedes the age of "dance set to music." The responsibility for this state of affairs must rest with choreographers, who demanded bland music for the simple reason that they did not know the meaning of musical specificity. Choreographers were accustomed to music that was bland and did not even imagine it could be otherwise: they filled it with mime and randomly chosen dance movements on the basis of melody and bar rhythm alone.

Petipa approached *The Sleeping Beauty* with the intention of using this time-honored method, but Tchaikovsky's music was written in a manner that precluded that possibility. Tchaikovsky invariably gave distinctive musical features to each of the characters in a ballet. Every single character in *The Sleeping Beauty* has his or her own musical theme (leitmotif).[23] In *The Sleeping Beauty,* there is no need to indicate entrances, characters, or scenes by means of instructions written on the score (a practice widespread in ballets of the age of "dance to the accompaniment of music"), because everything is made clear from beginning to end. In both mime and dance scenes, it is easy to identify the musical phrases that belong to particular characters; consequently, it is quite unacceptable to fill the music in a haphazard way, using the first dance movements that come to mind. However, Petipa clung to the old principles. He staged *The Sleeping Beauty* in exactly the same way he had staged his previous ballets. As a consequence, a musician who watches a performance of this or any other ballet by Tchaikovsky or Glazunov will be aware of the lack of correspondence between dance and music much more acutely than with ballets to music written by composers before Tchaikovsky.

The music of Tchaikovsky and his successors demands a totally new approach: if this fact is not recognized, all the tenets by which the art of choreography has always set such great store are undermined. As far as the music from the age of "dance to the accompaniment of music" is concerned, these tenets may have seemed somewhat esoteric, but for strictly symphonic music they barely suffice, as we can see even nowadays when a production to the new type of music is staged on the basis of principles from the age of "dance to the accompaniment of music." At the end of a ballet to the music of old-style composers, audiences leave the theater convinced that the balletic action and, in particular, the dance are at a significantly higher level of sophistication than the music to which they are set; by contrast, after a production where the music has been written by first-class symphonists, the departing public completely forgets the choreography, having been so impressed by the music, for the music is far superior to the dance that accompanies it.

I am deliberately stressing the "accompanying" nature of ballet music from the age of "dance to the accompaniment of music," because I wish to highlight that, in the new era that dawned with the music of Tchaikovsky, the "accompanying" role was transferred to dance. Though as a choreographer I am loath to admit it, the balance between dance and music shifted in favor of the latter as a direct result of the improvement in its quality. However, it is not difficult to rectify this unsatisfactory state of affairs. All that is required is a rejection of the principles that endorse the random selection of dance movements or mime gestures and the haphazard setting of these movements and gestures to music on the basis of the rhythms of the opening bars of the melody or phrase. To refuse to abandon the old principles is to leave choreography in an inglorious position and to sanction the unwelcome prolongation of the age of "dance set to music."

As proof of the bankruptcy of the old method of "filling up" the music in a random and chaotic way, I shall adduce some examples from the music and staging of *The Sleeping Beauty*. The first is the prelude to the entrance of the Lilac Fairy together with the entrance itself (see music example 12). In Petipa's choreography, neither of these sections stands out theatrically or choreographically, yet Tchaikovsky places strong emphasis upon this episode. By means of a key change during the Lilac Fairy's entrance,[24] he creates an atmosphere of joyous excitement, while at the same time distinguishing her entrance from that of the other fairies. Petipa's version has the fairies, headed by the Lilac Fairy, entering in an orderly procession; the

Пример № 7

Music example 12

key change for the Lilac Fairy's entrance is not echoed onstage, and consequently harmony and correspondence with the music are absent at this point. Petipa did not think that this section was important, yet Tchaikovsky, judging by the score, endows it with particular significance. Why? Because the appearance of the Lilac Fairy marks the starting point for the development of an important theme: the theme of a bright new beginning. I am stressing the failure to reflect this particular key change in theatrical and choreographic terms because such oversights are absolutely typical of all Petipa's productions and because true harmony and correspondence between dance and music are impossible while this kind of negligence is tolerated. I shall suggest ways by which harmony and correspondence may be achieved when I go on to discuss the integration of dance and music. The whole of the entrance of the fairies was completely mishandled by Petipa; his arrangement makes the fairies look as though they are on parade, following one another as for an inspection. The music makes it clear that the scene is part dance.[25] Tchaikovsky makes a clear distinction between the appearance of the guests at the ball and the appearance of the fairies, but Petipa ignores it. One might say that in Tchaikovsky's version the guests *arrive* and the fairies *appear*, whereas in Petipa's version both groups arrive. What we have here, of course, is an example of the old principles at work. The ballet music is simply filled in a haphazard way without any attempt to reflect the musical particularity of individual characters or situations. In applying this approach to the new music of Tchaikovsky, the beautiful scene in which the fairies appear is ruined. One cannot fail to see or feel the ill effects: the lack of correspondence between music and dance is glaringly obvious.

Let us now move on. I shall omit the dance section of the fairies' scene because it is constructed in exactly the same way as Albrecht's variation in Act II of *Giselle*, which I have already analyzed. In every variation, the movement of the dance is to a greater or lesser extent out of synchronization with the movement of the music. (As I have already suggested, when a dance is constructed on the basis of the melody and the meter,[26] it is

perfectly possible that harmony will sometimes occur coinci-
dentally or that there will be a temporary correspondence—
of no more that two or three bars' duration—between dance
and music.)

When we come to the entrance of the fairy Carabosse (see
music example 13), the pause is virtually ignored onstage. To
have Carabosse arrive at the ball in a carriage seems to me very
dubious;[27] the music does not suggest an arrival by carriage.
Here we have the appearance of an evil presence who looks
around to see what impression she has made upon those in the
room, and at this point there is a spiteful, watchful pause.
Petipa did not even notice it.

Пример № 8

Music example 13

I have chosen the next example (see music example 14)
because Petipa gives this and the following section exclusively
to Carabosse, with the King and Queen merely interrupting her
to say that Catalabutte is very forgetful. The music, however,
suggests something quite different. The first and second bars

Пример № 9

Music example 14

of music example 14 convey the final moment when the maliciously laughing Carabosse appears. The third and fourth bars (with the exception of the last quarter-bar) depict the King and Queen addressing Carabosse, who can barely contain her spiteful rage.[28] This is conveyed by the insistent triplets on the double basses that belong to Carabosse's theme. In the fourth quarter of the fourth bar and the first quarter of the fifth bar, there is an explosion of uncontrolled rage from Carabosse that cuts across the theme of the King and Queen. Subsequently, periodic recurrences of these outbursts break through to the surface. Thus, in the music, the theme of appeasement that belongs to the King and Queen is constantly cut short by the stormy flashes of Carabosse's theme, until in the end the latter dominates completely. The theme of the King and Queen is stifled and breaks off, finally allowing Carabosse's malice to be given free rein. Onstage, the whole episode is played as if it were in reverse. The malicious Carabosse is active the whole time, with the King and Queen offering only an occasional interruption. Petipa, casting a danseur in the role of Carabosse, gave him total freedom and disregarded the changing musical themes. Of all the artists I have seen dancing this role (Enrico Cecchetti, Alexander Shiryaev, Alexander Chekrygin, and Timofei Stukolkin),[29] only Chekrygin observed the differing themes and made an attempt to treat this section in the way Tchaikovsky intended. Unfortunately, he was hampered by Petipa's erroneous mise-en-scène. Here we have yet another error resulting from the old practice of "filling" the music in a haphazard way without interpreting it: the entire melody is given over to the whim, as it were, of a single character. It is only too easy to overlook the fact that one artist may be more musical than another; one dancer may notice a thematic shift, but another, being possessed of less musical talent, may not, even if he is a marvelous performer. The responsibility for all the misunderstandings that arise as a consequence of this must rest firmly with the ballet master who failed to draw attention to the musical theme changes in the first place.

It is worth pointing out again that, when composers like Tchaikovsky wrote music to accompany ballet, they invariably gave a typical musical color to each character. It is clear that the fourth quarter of the fourth bar and the first quarter of the fifth bar in our example must belong to Carabosse because they are based on the spiteful triplets we associate with her. Later, when she explodes with uncontrollable rage and the theme of the King and Queen is completely eclipsed, the same triplets serve as the introduction to the theme of her radiating anger (see music example 15). The B-flat major Garland Waltz in Act I provides a clear illustration of the consequences of treating the music of *The Sleeping Beauty* as if it were no different from the type of music that usually accompanied ballet (that is, setting dance movements to previously identified phrases and determining their rhythm on the basis of the first few bars).[30] It is obvious to me that the ballet master had already thought out the main figures before he even became properly acquainted with the music and devised and set the dance details during the actual staging in rehearsal, following his instinct. As a result, while the B-flat major waltz as a whole matches the musical meter, it is not at all well coordinated with the music as such: its separate constituent parts do not all contain the same number of bars in fact, even though it appears at first glance that all the melodies are based on eight or, less commonly, ten bars.

Пример № 10

Music example 15

Typically, the opening bars in the music (see music example 16) were ignored. These four bars serve as an introduction to the waltz itself. I would not even mention them if the choreographed waltz began at the same time as the melody that directly follows these four introductory bars. However, Petipa's waltz also has introductory bars: the balancé executed over the first sixteen bars following the four bars of the musical introduction is itself of an introductory nature. Thus, Petipa's introduction starts at the point where the musical introduction finishes, and the result is a glaring lack of correspondence between music and dance. Petipa set his dances to eight- or ten-bar sections he had identified in the melody. By using the balancé over the sixteen bars at the beginning of the waltz melody as a choreographic introduction and starting the dance proper in the second half of the first figure in the melody,[31] Petipa's choreography very quickly—after eight bars in the second half of the first figure—parts company with the music, for the movements remain the same even as the waltz melody is resolving into its second figure. Petipa's version of the second half of the figure is based on a single pattern, with the addition of two more bars—17 and 18—to which he does not set any dance movements at all. From the musical point of view, by contrast, the second half of the first figure (see music example 17) consists of four patterns that are musically distinct and lead unswervingly toward the second figure. If there is to be

Пример № 11

Music example 16

harmony and correspondence between music and dance, then the dance movements must also be distinct and lead toward the second figure. In Petipa's version, the first four bars contain a complete choreographic section that is repeated four times in the course of the musical segment shown in musical example 17. This is wrong, because in the ninth bar the shape of the melody dramatically changes. From bar 9 to the first quarter of bar 15, the music demands a new dance movement that is quite different from the movement of the first eight bars; the melodic structure is based on two beats, and the dance movement should reflect this.[32] Bars 15 and 16 are transitional, before the return of the three-beat measure displaced in bar 9; they should be accompanied by similarly transitional dance movements. Petipa effectively misses out bars 17 and 18: he fills them with balancés. Balancés might have been used to better effect in bars 15 and 16, where they would parallel the adjustment in the music. Bars 17 and 18 are in a firm and steady three-beat measure and mark a return to the starting point, as Tchaikovsky emphasizes by reinforcing the sound with a double forte. In this situation, a movement such as the balancé is totally inappropriate.

Having settled back into the movement of the waltz in bars 17 and 18 following the displacement in bar 9, Tchaikovsky uses exactly the same two bars six bars later for emphasis (see musical figure 18):[33] Petipa, on the other hand, having set a balancé to bars 17 and 18 (musical example 17), sets completely different movements for bars 1 and 2 of figure 18; in

Пример № 12

Music example 17

other words, he does not reproduce the musical repetition in choreographic terms. Petipa's staging is out of order both musically and rhythmically and serves only to confirm my opinion that the dance is put together in a random and chaotic way, using the first movements that occurred to him.

Petipa ran into all the trouble I have described because he thought that the waltz melody could be divided into equal sections of eight bars each. On a superficial level, that does indeed appear to be the case, but a more careful look reveals that some sections of the waltz melody are only six bars long.[34] I shall not pursue my analysis of the waltz any further: the lack of correspondence between the music and its figuration is constant. Having come to grief at the very outset, Petipa persisted with an arrangement that remains out of harmony with the music to the very end.

I am surprised to find that, even among musicians, there are those who defend the arrangement of the dances to the B-flat major waltz. I do not deny that it has an interesting figuration, but there are interesting figures in circus performances as well, and nowadays we regard these as nonrhythmic throwbacks to the principle of "dance with music." In fact, the staging of this waltz is quite similar to the staging associated with "dance with music": when the principle of "dance to the accompaniment of music" was applied to the music of Tchaikovsky—music that cannot under any circumstances be described as an "accompaniment to ballet"—the consequence was that the rhythmicity characteristic of accompanying music and the relative harmony between dance and music found in ballets preceding *The Sleeping Beauty* were actually reduced.

Пример № 13

Music example 18

Let us return to ballets with music in the role of accompaniment. An analysis of ballets from the age of "dance to the accompaniment of music" reveals an ever-increasing harmony between dance and music that reaches its peak in the staging of *Les Caprices du Papillon*, to the music of Nikolai Krotkov. This can be explained in the following way. From long experience, composers came to the realization that ballet masters paid little attention to their music and repeatedly worked against it. They therefore began to adapt their own creative work to accommodate dance, invariably following a single pattern for all ballets, regardless of whether the ballet was to be realistic or fantastic. They also realized that dance and mime scenes would always be staged on the basis of identifiable melodies and that the harder it was for the ballet master to find the melodies, the greater the chances of his rejecting the music. Consequently, music had to be written in such a way that the melodies stood out. No complex transitions, contrasts, interwoven sections, or conflicting musical themes were acceptable in view of the choreographers' ignorance of such devices and the consequent possibility that the music might be considered unsuitable for ballet. Cesare Pugni, who composed a great deal for ballet, was, of course, a trained musician. Without doubt, he could have written more complicated ballet music, but he knew perfectly well that if he did so, his music would be rejected because it would be incomprehensible and thus difficult to stage. Over a number of years, during which they wrote essentially the same music over and over, composers managed to adapt their work to the requirements of ballet masters, knowing in advance how the ballet would be staged and confident that the necessary harmony between music and dance would occur of its own accord. *The Little Humpbacked Horse*,[35] *La Bayadère*, and *The Daughter of Pharaoh* contain virtually the same tunes, but, in terms of rhythm and the harmony between dance and music, *La Bayadère* is an improvement on *The Daughter of Pharaoh* because the latter was an earlier work. Thus, yet again, progress came about not because of the ballet master's efforts but because the composer learned to adapt and "advance-guess"[36]—which was not difficult, because the staging of dance and mime scenes in the age of "dance set to music" was basically the same, whatever the ballet.

Ballet masters of that time and, consequently, the public, which took its cue from the ballet masters, were often heard to complain that music was "not danceable" or "not melodic." It is clear from these complaints exactly what kind of music supported ballet performances in the age of "dance to the accompaniment of music." Petipa had been brought up with the idea that ballet music could be disregarded, and he could see that he himself was achieving harmony and correspondence between dance and music (even if he forgot or, rather, did not even begin to imagine that this harmony was mainly the result of the composer's adaptability). However, when he applied his methods to Tchaikovsky's music, there was far less harmony between dance and music in the resulting production than there had been in *Les Caprices du Papillon,* which he had staged before *The Sleeping Beauty.*[37] Clearly, in the three months that separated these two productions, Petipa could not radically alter his approach to ballet music. Tchaikovsky, on the other hand, attempted, as he set about writing *The Sleeping Beauty,* to discover from Petipa exactly what was required of him but found himself quite unable to meet Petipa's demands. Only a composer who was aware of all the weak points in the relationship between choreography and music could have made the necessary concessions, and no composer would possess this awareness unless he worked for the administration of the Maryinsky Theater, where he would come into regular contact with choreography and be familiar with its needs.

All the trends that dominated choreography at that time were completely alien to Tchaikovsky. The composers who worked for the theater administration were barely aware of the fact that they were making adjustments to their work; they did it through force of habit. All ballet story lines and choreographic movements were essentially the same, as I have already said. Only the visual effects and the costumes changed. It was therefore easy to transfer an effective variation or even an entire dance from one ballet to another. I am inclined to think that, had Tchaikovsky known what compromises the other composers were making—albeit unconsciously—in order to improve performances overall, he would have refused to compose for ballet on the grounds that he could not possibly follow their example. Tchaikovsky wrote *The Sleeping Beauty* as a serious musician, devoting no less attention to it than he devoted to his symphonies and operas; in fact, if one or two extraneous variations are removed, the whole ballet is completely symphonic. Every character in the ballet is depicted musically by means of a leitmotif.[38] The leitmotif is developed musically in every way possible throughout the ballet. This feature alone makes considerable demands upon the ballet master, who had rarely, if ever, faced anything similar in the work of Tchaikovsky's predecessors. Not only does every character have his or her own musical physiognomy (both in the mime and in the dance scenes), but also he or she undergoes a purely musical development; therefore, the character and his or her development must be drawn choreographically, as well. If this problem is not properly addressed, there is an immediate lack of correspondence between music and dance. Both these features—the leitmotif and musical development—were introduced to ballet music by Tchaikovsky: neither of them should be ignored. And yet, when dance was staged "to the accompaniment of music," this was ignored for the simple reason that it was all completely unfamiliar as far as choreography was concerned. Having listened to Tchaikovsky's music, Petipa just brushed aside all the innovations and staged *The Sleeping Beauty* in the same way he had staged all his previous ballets. As a result, the lack of correspondence between dance and music became even more stark.

Tchaikovsky ushered in a new era in the writing of music for ballet. Thus, after the production of *The Sleeping Beauty,* choreography lost the commanding position it had occupied in relation to music, lost all it had gained in terms of harmony with music, and took up a subordinate role. The whole idea of special "danceable," melodic music for ballet was abandoned, and its place was taken by general rules of composition that applied to any music. With the first production of *The Sleeping Beauty*, choreography moved into a new, difficult, but necessary phase in its development, making the transition from "dance to the accompaniment of music" to "dance set to music." This is not dissimilar to "dance to the accompaniment of music," but, as a result of the refinement of music, choreography [in this phase] has moved into the background. There it will have to stay until its practitioners change the principles in accordance with which ballets are staged and which are based upon an ignorance of ever advancing, ever more complex musical forms.

The question arises as to whether choreography actually benefited from the improvement in ballet music—an improvement for which Tchaikovsky, through his refusal to accept the old concessionist methods, laid the foundation. Is it not possible that composers, by making even further adjustments, could have brought about a harmony between music and dance so close as to satisfy completely both musicians and choreographers? As a choreographer myself, I do not think so. I am forced to the conclusion that never under any circumstances could such a situation enable choreography to develop in the manner it deserves, for any joint progress would be entirely dependent upon the ability of composers to adapt (an unconscious ability in the majority of cases), while choreography and its principles would remain at a standstill. The only way forward from the present impasse is the way I described earlier: either composers must study choreography or ballet masters must study music. The latter is preferable, since the ballet master has an easier task than the composer. Perhaps we should accept the fact that the first performance of *The Sleeping Beauty* was a day of humiliation for choreography. Perhaps we should admit that choreography fell that day into a subordinate position. However, this setback, painful though it was, also served a positive purpose, for, with time, it enabled choreographers to seek out a new principle of staging: the principle of "the integration of dance and music," according to which choreography and music are of equal importance, with no pressure from either one on the other.

At the present time, the integration of dance with music has yet to become a reality; the few examples to be found are fortuitous. We are still firmly in the age of "dance set to music," but the desire to integrate dance and music exists alongside it and is already universally recognized, though it is rarely expressed openly. Neither musicians nor choreographers have put forward any specific ideas (by which I mean ideas that might help ballet masters to integrate dance with music), because there is no representative of either of the two arts with sufficient knowledge of the characteristics of both. My task is to express my own understanding of this matter, in the hope that my ideas may initiate the process of integrating dance and music.

I have already defined the ages of "dance with music," "dance to the accompaniment of music," and "dance set to music" in broad terms. These definitions will help us to define our new principle because we know that everything ballet masters *failed* to do in those ages, as revealed by our analysis, must be incorporated in the staging of productions based on the integration of dance and music. The integration of dance and music—what an alluring, yet dangerous object of desire! It is alluring if only because it has not yet been achieved, but also because those amazing, fleeting moments when a fragment of dance merges completely with the music, when dance and music speak the same language, are enough to convince us of the force of the union and consequently of the worthiness of bringing it about. The only danger is that, in striving to integrate dance and music, we mechanize dance by reproducing only the duration and tempo of the notes in the musical score.[39] This was what happened in the case of the system developed by Emile Jaques-Dalcroze. In my opinion, stage productions based upon his system are a total failure; I have never seen anything in the work of the followers of Dalcroze other than the use of arms and legs for the purpose of "reproducing notes." It was not only Dalcroze who came to grief in this way. So did all the others who, seeing that choreography had not succeeded in integrating dance and music, began to rant about its shortcomings in general and about the ballet productions at the Maryinsky

Theater in particular, claiming that they could solve all the problems on their own and rejecting out-of-hand the experience accumulated over the years choreography had been in existence. For my part, I shall always look upon the artists of the Maryinsky Theater[40] as the greatest representatives of the art of choreography, but all of those ranters who strode out ahead of the rest of us may be likened to the tom-tit in the Russian folktale who could not set fire to the sea:[41] their grand ambitions have come to nothing, as anyone who has an interest in choreography can clearly see.

We are choreography—we, the representatives of that art to be found in ballet productions on the stage of the Maryinsky Theater, we, even with all our faults. We are choreography, for no one else has achieved more in the field of choreography than we have. Of course, it is not wrong to notice defects, but neither is it difficult; what is infinitely more difficult is to eliminate those defects. All those who talk at such length about our faults are mistaken if they think we are unaware that we have any. We have always known perfectly well what our failings are, but we are not inclined to shout them from the rooftops. Instead, we would rather correct them quietly, as is evident from the various stages of dance that I have analyzed, each of which shows an improvement on the previous age.

The integration of dance and music cannot be achieved by the means at the disposal of our critics. I have not missed a single one of the dance productions put on by people who set out to prove that they could eliminate the defects found in our work, defects that at first glance seemed so easy to correct. But how painful the experience has been in every case! These performances purport to represent the new art of choreography, which lives in total harmony with music. But what poor and at times worthless devices these fledgling apostles of choreography present to us! None of them has mastered as much as 1 percent of the techniques available to choreography as represented by us. As long as all these demonstration performances remained within the sphere of character dance,[42] they were still just about watchable, although one could not fail to be aware of their

limited nature. However, as soon as the music required release
from the ground, the poverty and paucity of their resources
became obtrusively noticeable. Pathetic attempts were made at
rising to demi-pointe, when what was required was full pointe,
signifying complete separation from the ground. What I find
amusing in all this is that the most complex-sounding ultra-
modern music was used for these exercises, for the sole purpose
of showing that the new choreographers had "grown up," in
the sense that they had succeeded in understanding contemporary music and were now able to integrate dance with it. One
is tempted to conclude that the innovators were trying to draw
attention to the fact that they themselves were perfectly capable
of devising a choreographic illustration of the music of composers such as Debussy,[43] whereas in the Maryinsky Theater
even Pugni is performed "nonrhythmically." Perhaps it is true
that in Maryinsky productions there are sections of dance to the
music of Pugni that do not correspond to the music: there may
even be many such sections. However, there are two points to
be made here. First, the staging of dance to the music of Pugni
dates back to the age of "dance to the accompaniment of
music"; if we were to stage dances to Pugni's music today, we
would make fewer mistakes in terms of harmony and correspondence with the music. Second, in spite of all the errors, it
has still proved possible to achieve the closest harmony between
dance and music, both in the age of "dance to the accompaniment of music" and in the present age of "dance set to music,"
and there are examples (though admittedly few) to prove it.
By comparison, in productions by representatives of so-called
contemporary choreography to complex modern music, there
are infinitely more errors in terms of the harmony between
dance and music, because these "pioneers" simply do not possess sufficient means of expression.

Even we, with all the rich possibilities open to us, sometimes
feel out of our depth nowadays when we come to stage dance
to the latest music, and we therefore make a conscious decision
to let the music guide us. What, then, are we to make of the
vain attempts of the ranters and dilettantes to illustrate the very

complicated music of the new musical age? They are simply fraudulent. It is we who will achieve the integration of dance and music, we the educated, professional choreographers who have experienced the whole complex development of dance. No doubt, we shall begin with less difficult music, but, once we have learned, we shall be able to stage dances to more intricate music, as well, for (as I have already said) there are far greater resources available to us.

We recognize the difficulty of integrating dance with the music of contemporary composers, but we do not reject the possibility of experiments in this direction, for we have sufficient means at our disposal. For my part, I am convinced that, in order to improve the art of choreography and to secure for it its rightful place, we should turn back to Tchaikovsky. All the principles laid down in the period leading up to and including the age of "dance to the accompaniment of music" must be ruthlessly cast out, because ballet music no longer plays an "accompanying" role.

Before one sets out to stage a dance, one must first of all become thoroughly acquainted with the music intended for the production and study in detail all the musical forms it contains. This is vital for the following reason. Before Tchaikovsky, ballet music contained predominantly simple forms as a result of its readiness to accommodate dance. It was made up of dance-specific, closely rhymed schemas to which the epithet "danceable" very obviously applied and that lent themselves very readily to dance arrangements. This very simple music lacked the kind of features that we find in the single-theme form typified by the fugue, which is based on counterpoint, or in the more complicated form of the sonata, with its contrasting, interweaving, and opposing melodic strands. Can it be claimed that, from the time of Tchaikovsky onward, ballet music has been dominated by the ultrasimple, dance-specific, closely rhymed "danceable" form? Of course not. But, in that case, ballet music can no longer be approached using the same choreographic standards that prevailed before the time of Tchaikovsky.

The dance-specific form of music does not require any insights: everything about it is clear, everything is on display, there are no contrasting, interweaving, or opposing melodic strands. The whole is broken down into separate musical sections that are completely independent of one another and have nothing in common. It is only natural that, in the age when music of this sort was dominant, dance productions followed the same principle of "disconnectedness," and the various sections of the dance were quite unrelated. There was no question of an alternative, as we can see by examining any variation: the segments of dance are more often than not completely unconnected. Albrecht's variation from *Giselle* (musical examples 9, 10, and 11; pp. 115, 116, and 119), like all of Petipa's variations, was composed in accordance with a single plan that had become established over the years and was based on a very simple musical form; this was a very straightforward arrangement of dance sections consisting of unrelated parts and differing from each other only by virtue of the variety of their superficial prettiness.[44] Tchaikovsky, and all those who followed him in composing for choreographic productions, did not base their music on a single musical form but incorporated all existing musical forms irrespectively.

At this point, I have deliberately adopted the term "choreographic productions" in place of "ballet productions"; if it was once appropriate to describe a production based on a dance-specific form of music as "ballet" or "balletic," now that music for dance has become elevated to the point where it embraces all musical forms, the term "choreographic" is more accurate because it implies that the production includes all forms of movement and dance. This is by no means the definitive term: we need to find another designation that covers all varieties of musical and choreographic form and at the same time takes into account the narrative and theatrical nature of this type of production. The dance symphony is something else again.

After initial acquaintance with the music and a detailed search for and identification of its forms, it is no less important for the would-be choreographer to consider the color of the instrumentation, that is to say, to discover what instruments—one or many, string or wind—are used to put across particular focal points in the music. To this end, it is necessary to study the orchestral score in depth, for the score reveals all the thematic shifts from one instrument to another and makes it possible to determine the color and the force of the sound.[b]

In the process of staging productions that integrate dance and music, it is also important to ensure not only that audible emotional climaxes in the music coincide with visible emotional climaxes in the dance but also that the curve of the musical movement is matched by the curve of the dance movement. At this juncture, I should explain in greater detail what I envisage when I speak of concord between the sound curve and the dance curve. Obviously, when I say that the two should resemble each other, I do not just mean that "tapering" sounds (by which I mean sounds that seem to move upward from a lower starting point) should be matched by comparable movements on the stage. If that were all that was meant by concord, we would end up with dancers "making notes" with their feet, which is where the systems of Dalcroze and all his followers foundered, because invariably they abandoned the art of dance for dull rhythmic gymnastics. I, on the other hand, believe that choreography offers countless possibilities for achieving complete union between dance and music, none of which will lead to the pitfall of gymnastics.

Petipa, because he was not thinking about concord between the two lines of dance and sound, erred in the two bars from *The Sleeping Beauty* (see musical example 19)[45] only insofar as he failed to pay attention to the second half of the first bar, which appears to be similar to the first half but in fact contains more movement. The reason for this is that the notes in the second half of the bar are not staccato. The staccato hints at a certain statuelike quality, whereas the legato of the second half of the first bar implies an intensification of movement; the effect of its gentle forward progression is to ensure that the staccato

b. See the chapter on "The Ballet Master and the Score."

notes in the second bar convey a statuelike stillness even more strongly.

In the first two semiquavers of the first bar, Petipa has the danseuse rise from fifth position to pointe on her right foot, with the left leg suspended in midair in an attitude effacé. During the next two semiquavers she returns to fifth position with the other foot in front.[46] Throughout, Petipa requires precision as well as stillness. This is undoubtedly correct, for the notes E, G, A, and B are essentially static here. The upward turn in the sound is reflected in the dance in that the movements I have described advance forward and to the side; although not an exact match for the music, they are sufficiently close to it. Likewise, the supplementary attitude effacé can be regarded as a movement with upward progression, so it too is true to the music. However, in the second half of the bar, Petipa makes his mistake. He has the danseuse perform an almost exact repetition of the movements I have just outlined, but starting with the other foot in front and sur le cou-de-pied front in place of the attitude effacé. Petipa completely loses sight of the effect of the legato on the notes in this part of the bar. The closest harmony between this section of the music and the dance movements could have been there for all to see if Petipa had made the danseuse perform sur le cou-de-pied with a pirouette en dedans. This combination would have properly conveyed the upward-moving legato in the music: the pirouette, or turn on one leg, is essentially a gentle movement, especially the pirouette en dedans.

Пример № *i*,14

Music example 19

From all that has been said about the correspondence between
the curve of the movement of the dance and the curve of the
movement of the sound, it should be obvious that it is by no
means essential to choreograph dance steps that involve movement up and down the stage at points where the music goes up
or down. Choreographers are capable of devising movements
that can be executed in situ but that convey the impression
of movement up, side, back, and down. The musical line can
show movement up, down, and to the side, effort that is slow
or energetic, equilibrium, stability, or motionlessness in varying
degrees of intensity; so can the dance line. When the musical
line speaks of upward flight, concern as to whether the dance
movements fit the musical measure must not be allowed to
override other considerations to the extent that a contradiction
arises between music and dance.

Let us take the grande pirouette—an amazing movement on
account of its peculiar centrifugal energy—as an example. The
line of this superhuman movement may suggest a paroxysm, a
whirlwind, or something similar, but under no circumstances
can it be conjoined with the rhythmic pattern and down-to-
earth melody of a march. However, even now, this dance movement, which has nothing down-to-earth about it, nearly always
appears in a male variation in the coda of a pas de deux, where
it is set to march music with a closely rhymed melody.[47] Viewed
from the point of view of the ideal—the integration of dance
and music—this is a major error. The movement is set to the
two-beat measure of the march because of the way in which
the supporting foot touches the ground; however, the power of
this movement is not in the supporting foot but in the centrifugal force generated during the turn by the leg extended
to the side. I know of only one example of the correct use of
this movement, and that is in the coda of Harlequin's variation
from Schumann's *Carnaval,* as choreographed by Fokine.[48]
Here it is used to depict a paroxysm of joy and laughter and is
closely conjoined with the music. The fouetté turn is comparable to the grande pirouette.

Any examination of the fundamental elements in the integration of dance and music would be incomplete without a discussion of the analogy between major and minor in music and en dehors and en dedans in dance, these being formed from the static effacé and croisé poses. Effacé creates openness of movement within a static context; en dehors creates a similar openness but within a dynamic context. Croisé creates a "crossed," "closed" movement within a static context; en dedans creates a dynamic, closed movement. The associations of effacé with "openness" and croisé with a "crossed" or "closed" position come from Volynsky,[49] and I entirely agree with them; however I cannot agree with the comments he makes in one of his articles in the journal *Zhizn' iskusstva* (The Life of Art) to the effect that croisé and effacé are dance positions and therefore dynamic. It is impossible to dance effacé and croisé because effacé and croisé are essentially static. Their dynamic variants are effacé en dehors and croisé en dedans.

To return to the analogy between major and minor on the one hand and en dehors and en dedans on the other, I shall now examine each in turn in order to show how major relates to en dehors and minor to en dedans. The musical major is clear and bright and corresponds exactly to the open form "en dehors," for clarity and brightness are essentially the same as "openness." Minor, by contrast, is melancholy and clouded and consequently corresponds to the "crossed," closed en dedans form, for melancholy can be expressed only by closed movement. It follows from this that the process of arranging dance movements necessarily involves taking account of the key—major or minor—in which the music is written so as to avoid a discrepancy between the music and the dance. Obviously, the major mode will manifest itself in movements en dehors and the minor mode in movements en dedans.

In music, the juxtaposition of major and minor can be used to create a wide variety of impressions. It stands to reason that en dedans and en dehors must replace each other only at points where major changes to minor or vice versa. The collocation of major and minor aside, it must not be forgotten that it is possible to reinforce an impression by the choice of a particular key from the total of twenty-four, twelve of which are major and twelve minor. This is important, because it has been shown that, while all the major keys are similar in that they are all essentially light and joyful, they differ in color, each being of a different intensity. Key changes, therefore, are of considerable relevance in the staging of dance. In music, a change of key is achieved through modulation. Therefore, there must also be modulation in dance, though, as I have said before, it is usually omitted, despite the fact that it serves as a connecting link between different keys. The entrance of the Lilac Fairy in Act I of *The Sleeping Beauty* provides a good illustration of the need to emphasize musical key changes by choreographic means[50] (musical example 12; p. 125). The appearance of the Fairy is in no way accentuated, and consequently her stage entrance is pale by comparison with her musical entrance. It would be easy to equalize the two, if only by means of a sudden change in the grouping of all those already onstage. As long as the ballet master pays attention to the key change, the changes in the grouping will suggest themselves to his imagination of their own accord. As for choreographic modulation, even that need not prove too difficult if it is constructed in the same way as musical modulation is constructed, by adding a part of the new theme to a part of the old theme and gradually transforming the old into the new. Obviously, this is possible only if one abandons once and for all the practice of filling music in a haphazard way with the first dance movements that come to mind.

The integration of dance and music depends primarily upon the development of choreographic themes, but it also hinges upon the fundamental rules set out here. A ballet or dance symphony must be constructed in accordance with the following rules:

1. The work must be based upon the elaboration of choreographic themes that conflict, contrast, and develop in

parallel with each other; it must not be based upon a random selection of dance movements.

2. Choreographic and musical themes must work together, not cut across each other. For example, a musical theme that suggests upward flight cannot be combined with a choreographic theme that suggests crawling, even if the two themes are identical in terms of rhythm.

3. There must be both metric and thematic rhythmicity (correspondence between dance and music).

4. Ballet mime, where each gesture signifies a word plucked at will from the music, must be eliminated. Old balletic gestures must be replaced by gestures that are strictly in accordance with the music, reflect its character, and express not just a single word but the meaning of an entire phrase.

5. There must be a unity of the musical and choreographic forms.

6. Emotional climaxes in the dance must coincide with emotional climaxes in the music.

7. The curve of the dance must correspond to the curve of the music.

8. The color of the dance movements must match the color of the orchestration.

9. Major keys must be equated with en dehors and minor with en dedans.

10. Key changes must be reproduced choreographically.

11. Musical and choreographic nuances must be consonant.

12. Ethnic dance movements must be based upon the characteristic national gait that has developed as a consequence of the features of the natural environment of a given people.[c]

---

c. See part 3 below on ethnic dance movements. [Ed. note: The twelfth and last item in Lopukhov's list is of a different order from the others and has nothing to do with relationships between dance and music. As the footnote indicates, perhaps it was introduced as a link with the series of chapters (part 3) that immediately follows.]

Conclusion

What emerges from all that I have set out in this book? First of all, a number of conclusions may be drawn that I hope will assist ballet masters in their staging of ballets, dance symphonies, and national dances. It is time to abandon once and for all the practice of filling a piece of music to which dance is to be performed with the first movements that come to mind without regard for their appropriateness. It is time to treat audiences with greater respect, but at the same time we need to teach these audiences to look properly at a form of creative work they dismiss as rubbish for no other reason than that they do not understand it. Perhaps the chapters in *The Ballet Master and His Art* do not provide sufficiently clear answers to all the questions that arise—doubt may creep in at certain points—but there is enough in what I have said that *will* prove acceptable, that *will* be borne out in practice, indeed is already being borne out, to justify my undertaking. We must conscientiously piece together all the fragments that will pave the way for the recognition of the art of dance, for dance really is a great art, even if it has not yet found its true voice or been properly acknowledged. For my part, I ask no more than that what I have said about the art of choreography and the opportunities it offers be considered significant, if only as a small piece of the whole mosaic.

A second matter connected with the theme of this book, and no less important than the first, is the whole issue of criticism. Before I address the subject of dance criticism, I should point out that in fact there is no such thing in Russia.[a1] The art of choreography, having arrived at the "grotesque" stage[2]— fantastically complex dance movements that are beyond class and nationality, based upon the soft plié, and involving thematic choreographic development—is still without any form of criticism. It is true that a great deal is written about the success or failure of this ballet production or that particular artist, but criticism in general does not exist. Moreover, what is written is fundamentally lacking in seriousness. It is simply positive or negative comment without any coherent evaluation of the individual performance or the production under scrutiny; it is no more than a set of personal impressions, some of which are even based on personal relationships. Contemporary ballet critics at best remind me of the proprietors of antique shops who through their proximity to works of art have developed a practiced eye but who lack any real knowledge. For proof of this claim, one only has to look at arts such as music or painting as a comparison. One would be hard pressed to find a single music critic who had not studied music, even if only as a dilettante. The same is true of art critics. The reason may be that, by the time they finish their secondary education, future critics have achieved their general school certificates in all subjects, including art and music, even if they have reached only a minimum level of attainment. Dance critics, on the other hand, approach this greatest of arts with no knowledge whatever, not even an elementary acquaintance with the five basic positions,

a. This remark does not apply to Akim Volynsky, the only dance critic who approaches his task in the proper way. He was the first to counter Serge Volkonsky's claim in the press that all dance movements are without significance. His view that the classical adagio was a development of the growth process in plants seems to me to offer the only correct and useful explanation of the adagio's origins. Volkonsky's opinions are superficial, the result of ignorance of the subject. Volynsky has studied dance and has realized that the classical dance, one of the highest forms of the art of dance, could not have reached its present heights if it had not contained within itself the seed of life. I am in total agreement with Volynsky's views on the essence of the classical dance; we differ only in the details.

for the five positions are not taught in any educational institutions apart from professional dance academies.[3]

I am astonished that this unsatisfactory state of affairs has not been rectified. There is no doubt that dance exercise at a young age can correct many deficiencies of the human figure and gait. A study of the art of choreography is not only for devotees. Dance as a form of exercise is as essential in all secondary educational institutions as any other subject, for it enables the individual to develop an awareness of his or her human particularities. Those who have a real talent for it may pursue the subject further and make the most of their abilities, but a basic knowledge of choreography should be compulsory for everyone, as is a basic knowledge of any other subject. Until the study of the fundamentals of the art of dance becomes compulsory in secondary schools, we cannot expect to see the emergence of a proper dance critic.

Words cannot express the feeling one experiences when performing even the most simple dance movements, right down to the five basic positions. In order to be able to understand these positions, and hence to understand the art of choreography itself—for the five positions are the choreographic equivalent of the scale in music or the line in painting—one must first of all be capable of performing them. Only then is one able to comprehend dance movements in general, for every dance movement includes one of the five positions, just as every musical work has a scale and every drawing contains a line. I am told by the dancer and teacher Agrippina Vaganova[4] that, when he was already fairly advanced in years, Volynsky studied for a time with Nicolas Legat and underwent a certain amount of classical ballet training. Volynsky understood that without a knowledge of the classical exercises, without an awareness of how dance movements feel, he would never be a good dance critic; hence, albeit late in the day, he set about acquiring at least a part of what would enable him to carry out his task properly.

What a mockery it is to write about the art of choreography, which is based upon the five positions, without even knowing what these positions are! Imagine the outcry if a leading light in the field of choreography who happened to have an interest in surgery and had observed a number of operations over the years took it into his head to write about a particular surgeon holding his lancet the wrong way or not treating his patient properly. I use this example because some critics justify themselves by saying, "I have been watching ballet for over ten years! I have seen Zucchi, Legnani, Sokolova![5] I know the names of all the ballet movements!" This is precisely the sort of outdated attitude I have been talking about. Although a critic of this ilk may recognize the name of a movement and indeed the movement itself, he will never be in a position to know whether or not it is performed properly. (Music is not the same. In music, it is easy for a critic to point out a mistake.) I am not denying that these individuals have a love of dance, but I cannot tolerate their professorial tone, which at the best of times is founded upon a misunderstanding. It is unheard of for anyone to write about a particular subject just because he feels like doing so. In any case, such a person would find it impossible, because his ignorance would immediately be apparent. Unfortunately, the situation in relation to dance is rather different. Here we often find individuals in the role of critic who only yesterday were barely aware that choreography existed. Someone who cannot even demonstrate the first position to a child, let alone correct the child's mistakes, writes articles claiming that this or that was performed imperfectly, that it was not pleasing to the eye, that a dancer's spine or arm was incorrectly positioned in a pirouette, that a head did or did not turn as it should. Because they do not understand what dancing on pointe is all about, people write passionate articles about "toes of steel," thereby doing scant justice to the fundamental characteristics of the classical dance, which are its weightlessness and ethereality.

If that is how matters stand, why do I not simply make a public announcement to the effect that most of what passes for dance criticism is in fact anything but that? For two reasons. The first is that the number of devotees to our form of art is relatively small, and our voices are lost in the milieu in which we currently find ourselves. Only those who have studied at a professional school have the slightest knowledge of dance. As a consequence, when someone writes an article about dance, everyone else believes what he says, except, of course, for us few devotees. The second reason is that, too often, we keep silent. We have a negative side to our nature. However small our numbers, if we really wanted to be heard, we could undoubtedly make ourselves heard, but the real question is whether we are prepared to do what is necessary. We must reject all superfluous reviews, all unnecessary publicity written by persons ignorant of choreography, because until we do we shall have to suffer the intrusion into our sphere of those who know next to nothing about it. Every artist likes to receive favorable notices, even when he or she is fully aware that the writer of the complimentary review does not know the first thing about choreography. It is difficult to imagine any performer rejecting praise of this sort. (Would one place an announcement in the press stating that a performance was in fact substandard?) But, by taking such a courageous step, the artist would kill two birds with one stone: the critic would lose his authority, and our art would be free of the publicity-seeking performer, because the ability to recognize our own failings prevents us from putting on airs. Every artist knows perfectly well whether his performance was good or bad, but he knows it because of his knowledge of choreography, not because of the public's favorable reaction or because of a success that may be undeserved.

We have all come across "professionals" who can make an artist successful, and we know how difficult it is for an artist to resist the temptation and to reject unwarranted praise for the sake of art. But, once an artist has accepted the praise—and it is usually with praise that the fledgling critic starts—he has effectively testified that the critic understands choreography. There is a tacit agreement between the critic and the performer. However, the accord is rather shaky because it is based solely upon praise; the critic has only to give the performer an unfavorable review for the contract to be broken, whereupon the performer claims quite without embarrassment that the critic in question does not understand choreography because he is not in possession of the necessary knowledge. The critic can then counterattack. He can point out that the performer has accepted his accolades in the past and, by so doing, has tacitly acknowledged his understanding of choreography. As a result, the stigma attaches itself not to the critic but to the performer who was willing to accept unwarranted praise in the first place. We must steer clear of needless publicity. We must be pure in relation to our art, and we must dispassionately reject praise that is unmerited; if we do otherwise, our art will not forgive us. Art has a stern custodian in the form of time. There are many cases of reviews that have exaggerated the merits of an artist to an unjustified degree; then one day everything comes crashing down, and the artist vanishes without trace. Art, through its guardian, time, ruthlessly shatters our castles in the air, but the memory of the true creative artist never dies, and his work will easily outlive malicious critics who themselves inhabit castles in the air.

I repeat: there is no such thing today as a true dance critic; there are only the reports of ballet performances based upon the personal opinions and taste of observers who write with none of the appropriate seriousness. In the meantime, we professionals impatiently await the appearance of a critic who possesses knowledge of the art of choreography and is free from prejudice. We cannot and will not accept present-day criticism, which in our view does no more than provide a survey of stage performances. When a reviewer attempts to penetrate the essence of choreography, revealing in the process the true depth of his ignorance, we protest. The critic of the future will have to know as much about choreography as we do and more about everything else. He must be able not only to point out an error but also to correct it; he must make comments that are more specific than "the ballerina was good," "the ballerina was appalling," or "the danseur displayed his choreographic mediocrity." It seems to me that remarks of this sort merely underscore the mediocrity of contemporary dance criticism, which until very recently has enjoyed its own special privilege of being inviolable in that it has deprived artists of any opportunity to defend themselves from even the most ill-founded and unsubstantiated attacks.[b]

My third point is addressed to the government. Perhaps we are mistaken, but, in view of the growing number of attacks on choreography that have appeared in the press recently, I and many other representatives of the art of choreography have formed the opinion that, in the eyes of the authorities, ballet is a flower cultivated by the bourgeois system, a flower that is both useless in itself and also alien to the new, quantitatively greater class of the proletariat that took up its position on a level with all other classes at the time of the Revolution. However, this view is based upon a misunderstanding. Man's primeval gestures, which gradually developed into modern stage mime and simultaneously gave rise to folk dance, which in turn matured into the high art of classical dance, are the core of the art that goes by the name of ballet. This art is the property of all mankind; it has elevated itself over the long period of its existence to the point where it can express the most abstract philosophical ideas, just as primitive dance conveyed the first impressions of life.

I cannot be persuaded that the art of choreography, with classical dance at this pinnacle, is superfluous. If it were, then by the same token we would also have to reject the art of music in its highest form, the symphony. Poetry, which has developed from and is the highest form of song, would likewise become superfluous, as would all the highest forms of all the arts. When it is said that any attempt to disseminate free thought through classical dance is pointless, I, being a representative of the art of ballet and therefore aware of all that it offers in its most perfect form, must leap to its defense, for there is no doubt that only music in aural terms and choreography in visual

b. I have in mind the scandalous ruling of the Imperial Theaters in the prerevolutionary period to the effect that an artist in the employ of one of its units could not reply to or defend himself against whatever nonsense appeared in the periodical press. It is only in the past decade that ways around this ruling have been found.

terms are capable of providing a dynamic interpretation of infinitely free thought.

Classical dance is essentially classless and international and expresses otherworldliness and lightness of being. Choreography's most perfect form, the "dance symphony," is based upon classical dance. Choreography thus provides all the necessary means for the full and varied expression of free thought. I believe that the negative view of classical dance as being irrelevant to the new social order is largely a consequence of ignorance of the art and its potential and can therefore be easily overturned. In this connection, the practice of putting on performances that are accessible and free to all is greatly to be welcomed, in that it provides the masses with the opportunity to become acquainted with the wonderful characteristics of classical dance. National folk dances are also being presented onstage, and this is also welcome: clearly, it is essential to cultivate these dances. Cities relentlessly devour national characteristics and will eventually swallow them up altogether; in the future the only visible record of the gradual development of different nations and the various stages of that development will be from choreographic representations on the stage. *Choreographic theater is a museum, a school, and a laboratory of the dance, an interpretation of the past and of all that human thought has to offer in the future.* There is no need to justify the choreographic representation of rituals from times long past. All ritual songs of all times and all peoples revolve to a greater or lesser degree around dance.[c] The recreation of ritual songs and ritual dances onstage constitutes, first, a means of preserving forever a memorial to antiquity and, second, a form of education, for a comparison of these preserved rituals with the

c. Alexander Afanasiev, "The Slavs' Poetic View of Nature"; Yevgeny Anichkov, "Ritual Spring Songs in the West and among the Slavs." [Ed. note: The full references are as follows: Alexander Nikolayevich Afanasyev, *Poeticheskiye vozzreniya slavyan na prirodu*, 3 vols. (Moscow: K. Soldatenkov, 1865–1869); Yevgeny Anichkov, "Vesennyaya obryadovaya pesnya na zapade i u slavyan" ("Ritual Spring Songs in the West and among the Slavs"), *Sbornik otdeleniya russkago yazyka i slovesnosti* 74, no. 2 (1903), 78, no. 5 (1905).]

rituals currently in existence, be they Christian or otherwise, provides a clear picture of the stages in the transformation of pagan rituals and the application of the latter to Christian ideology.[d] The Russian operas *Ruslan and Ludmila* by Glinka and *Mlada* and *The Snow Maiden* by Rimsky-Korsakov,[6] which are based exclusively on ritual song, will be seen in their true light only when they are staged by a choreographer. The recreation of the distant past as embodied in ritual song, with or without dance, is impossible for anyone except exponents of the art of choreography, for, without considerable knowledge and lengthy choreographic experience, it would be inordinately difficult to recreate the lost ritual movements whose existence is indicated by the words of the song. All attempts to do so without the assistance of a choreographer/ballet master have ended and will always end in failure. For a striking illustration of this point, one has only to compare Fokine's exceptionally faithful staging of Gluck's opera *Orfeo*[7] with productions of the same opera by individuals who are not choreographers.

Without wishing to deny the huge potential of the classical dance, I must admit that the outlook of today's ballet masters has, to some extent, failed to keep pace with the events of the past fifteen or twenty years. They still cling to a romanticism that is now played out. But this is a temporary phenomenon. If the praises of all the recent achievements of human reason must be sung from the stage—and I have no misgivings about this—then I would argue that only choreography, with the aid of classical dance in concord with music, is equal to the task. There is much to indicate that the art of choreography is being reborn. The Revolution has not destroyed it and cannot destroy it. What the Revolution has done is to lift all the dust that had settled over it. Our task is to ensure that the dust does not settle again, so that all may see the essence of our great and eternal art.

d. For example, Alexander Famintsin's research on the skomorokhs—wandering minstrels—in ancient Rus would come alive if the skomorokh style were reproduced onstage. [Ed. note: The full reference is: Alexander Sergeyevich Famintsin, *Skomorokhi na Rusi* (St. Petersburg, 1889).]

Choreographic Revelations

Contents of *Choreographic Revelations*

The following list of contents of *Choreographic Revelations* locates the two essays selected for translation within the book as a whole. The introduction to the book is by Galina Dobrovolskaya, author of the seminal book *Fedor Lopukhov* (Moscow–Leningrad: Iskusstvo, 1976). *Choreographic Revelations* falls into two sections; the first deals with choreography and analyzes elements of the repertory, and the second deals with the work of the ballet master as a creative artist or rehearsal director and with performance issues. Dobrovolskaya suggests that *Choreographic Revelations* represents a continuation of *The Ballet Master and His Art* but that it deals in greater depth with a narrower range of problems. She also points out that the book is aimed at the younger generation of ballet masters, while also being accessible to the ballet enthusiast. The titles of the translated chapters are followed by an asterisk.

Petipa as Creator of Choreographic Compositions in Sonata Form

When I talk about the duet and the pas de deux,[1] I feel I must describe, if only briefly, those of Petipa's choreographic compositions—from the pas de deux to the pas classique and from the duet to the grand pas—that I still remember, though without going into details of all the individual forms and structures. I am well aware that the information I am able to provide is incomplete. Still, it should convey at least a partial impression of Petipa's works.

I shall begin with the pas de deux in which I myself danced in 1901 when I was fourteen, as part of a school production. I rehearsed it with another pupil, Soboleva,[2] but just before the performance she was taken ill, and Georgievskaia[3] took her place. The performance was given in the former Maryinsky Theater, although previous productions of this nature had always taken place in the school theater, which now bears the name of Shiryaev.[4] My teacher, Nicolas Legat,[5] demonstrated the pas de deux to my partner and me. Legat said at the time that he had asked Petipa to recommend a piece that would be within the capabilities of the students. Petipa had suggested this particular pas de deux, composed some time previously, and had shown it to Legat. Here (see music example 20) is the

Music example 20

beginning of the melody that accompanies it (I have forgotten the original key, so I have written it in G major):[6] Petipa had composed this pas de deux as a young man. It was typical of so-called pure dance. I shall outline the movements from which it is constructed in the order in which they occur.

The beginning of this pas de deux is a sort of classroom exercise. Both performers execute a grand plié, which is typical of early Petipa and the period when "pure dance" came into being. Attitudes, poses à la seconde, glissades, and various sissonnes fondues follow. Then the danseuse takes an écarté effacé[a] pose while the danseur holds her, but not by the waist: he runs from one side to the other, catching her alternately by the right and the left hand, while she continues to stand in her écarté pose.

It is already clear from the above that this pas de deux was constructed completely differently from modern pas de deux, where supporting holds and vertical lifts predominate. Petipa's pas de deux was primarily a dance of slow turns and various pas de bourrées with changing poses. Nowhere did the danseur lift his partner into the air; the dance was for the most part a dance on the ground.

In its second section, the pas de deux develops through jetés, small ones at first, then larger ones. Then come the variations and the coda, consisting mainly of sauts de basques and more of the same jetés.

Subsequently, I myself made use of the opening grand plié in my *Dance Symphony*,[7] about which I have written on many occasions. I do not think that borrowing is a sin in circumstances where it is justified. Tchaikovsky appropriated Grétry's melodies for the minstrels' chorus in the second act of *The Maid of Orleans*,[8] actually noting that he had done so on the score. Borrowing becomes plagiarism only when what is borrowed is used without a proper understanding of its meaning and is then passed off as the borrower's own.

a. In fact, Vaganova's description of écarté effacé and croisé is not quite accurate because there is no "crossing over," which is the essential feature of croisé. [Ed. note: The provenance of the Agrippina Vaganova (1879–1951) description is uncertain.]

But let us return to Petipa. The pas de deux I have just described shows particularly clearly the direction in which Petipa was moving in relation to "pure dance"—from the pas de deux to the pas classique. If we look no further than Petipa's pas de deux, we can already see how their form gradually becomes more complex as overhead lifts begin to be introduced into the adagios.

The next oldest of Petipa's works is, I believe, the pas de deux in the first act of *Giselle*.[9] It is possible that this long-existent pas de deux was composed by Petipa under the influence of his predecessors. Here, too, vertical lifts are absent, but there are more complex supporting holds. For example, the danseuse executes two pirouettes on pointe, but the preparation for these is not from the usual fourth or fifth position. Instead, she drops to one knee, as a result of which the danseur cannot place his hand on her waist in advance. In circumstances like these, supporting holds require almost acrobatic skill and are at the very limit of what is possible. Vertical lifts are the obvious next step in the progression.

A pas de trois by Petipa in similar mode has been inserted into the first act of *Paquita*.[10] This pas de trois is of no significance as far as the line of the narrative is concerned. In the past, if one of the three performers fell ill unexpectedly, the pas de trois was simply omitted from the ballet. The vertical lift in this pas de trois is an indication of the emergence of new principles in the composition of choreographic ensembles. Audiences and artists alike regarded this lift as an innovation. (The danseuse who was lifted off the ground was specially selected for her intrepidity.)

It was *Paquita* that established the vertical lift as a new choreographic feature of narrative as well as "pure dance." In the first act, the way the ballerina was supported by her partner was justified by the fact that the heroine was a Spanish gypsy dancer performing in front of guests. The support was particularly striking because it was not a mythical being who was thus elevated but a real woman.

In general terms, the subject matter of *Paquita* does not bear close scrutiny. The heroine is the daughter of a count. At the instigation of the Governor, who for some reason is taking revenge on her father, she is stolen away in childhood by some gypsies and becomes a dancer. The hero is a hussar, and the whole ballet is a kind of admiring tribute to the officers of the hussars. The story is a typical tale of villainy; indeed, the only positive characters are Paquita and the hussar who falls in love with her (though it must be said that, in Act II, when Paquita saves her lover from a malicious attack, all performers are allowed some lighter dance episodes that show them to less disadvantage).

However, despite the trite libretto, *Paquita* was redeemed by the extra pas de trois and the splendid choreographic composition of the pas classique in the last act. Both pieces are devoid of narrative content; in both, the dance develops in accordance with its own laws. The pas classique is a classical symphony of dance; no one has ever surpassed Petipa in the creation of this form.

At this point, I should mention the fact that three variations were removed from the *Paquita* pas classique. They were taken out when the pas was restored for a production by the Maly Opera and Ballet Theater in Leningrad[11] and replaced by three others of little value. In these three variations, Petipa created dramatic, lyrical, and comic moods one after the other. The first variation, to a solo violin, was dramatic and willful; Vaganova danced it well, as did Tamara Karsavina, though in a more feminine style. The second, to the accompaniment of a harp, was lyrical; Lubov Egorova performed it beautifully. The third—comic, terre-à-terre, a sort of choreographic scherzo— was splendidly executed by Elsa Will.[12] The removal of these variations had an adverse effect on the content of Petipa's masterpiece and inflicted irreparable damage upon choreography.

No list of Petipa's greatest ensembles would be complete without the Pas de Diane from *Esmeralda*.[13] Vaganova's subsequent adaptation of this pas rendered it completely meaningless. Vaganova removed the part of the Satyr, thereby eliminating the conflict between Endymion and the Satyr that is the culmination of the whole ensemble; as a result, the work lost its narrative and choreographic harmony. I remember Petipa's Satyr well, as danced first by Georgy Kiaksht and later by Leonid Leontiev. The Satyr's leg jerked as if to kick away Endymion (originally Vaslav Nijinsky) who leapt over him in a soubresaut, while Diana (Anna Pavlova) took flight in jetés.[14] Together, the three enacted an unforgettable choreographic masterpiece. Alas, Petipa's masterpiece was distorted by Vaganova, who failed to realize that the whole of Petipa's Pas de Diane was brilliantly infused with the conflict between these characters.

To continue our analysis of Petipa's work, let us next examine the pas de cinq in the ballet *The Daughter of Pharaoh*.[15] Unfortunately, this celebrated grand adagio has been completely lost; none of those who performed it are still alive except Mathilde Kchessinska[16] and Egorova, and they are now living in Paris. Of course, the best way to preserve choreographic masterpieces would be to record them on film, but in the case of *The Daughter of Pharaoh* it is already too late for that. The grand adagio has sunk into oblivion, and, although I can attempt to describe it, I am constrained by the limits of my memory and my abilities as a writer.

On the whole, it is true to say that *The Daughter of Pharaoh*, a fairy-tale ballet,[17] is completely undeserving of attention. I would regard it as a piece of fairy vulgarism. The music is worse than second-rate: it is fit only for an equestrian display in a circus. And yet, buried amid all the music-and-dance rubbish is a pure diamond: the grand adagio. Paradoxically, the critics did not single it out for comment, even though some of them, such as Sergei Khudekov,[18] went into raptures over the ballet as a whole.

According to the poster for the ballet, there were six participants in this ensemble—the Pharaoh's daughter Aspicia, her friend and attendant Ramseya, two nameless female friends, a nameless male who may be a friend or a slave, and, of course, the hero, a traveler who in an opium dream has taken on the form of an Egyptian enamored of the daughter of the Pharaoh. The nameless characters do not play any part in the rest of the ballet. The whole structure of the adagio closely resembles that of the sonata form, with its opening, development, and finale-coda.[19] This is particularly significant in view of the fact that the music itself is not in sonata form.

This adagio is a work of pure dance. The narrative of the ballet is not furthered by it in any way (as it is, for example, by the pas d'action in Act II of *Raymonda*[20] or the duet in Act II of *Swan Lake*).

The ensemble cannot properly be called a pas de six because the sixth person—the hero himself—does not participate in it in a choreographic sense but simply walks about the stage. Petipa based the work upon the movements and groupings of five performers. Not only does the sixth, the hero of the ballet, have no choreographic part to play, he is actually superfluous. As a rule, the audience did not even notice this sixth performer (offensive as this must have been to such an eminent soloist as Pavel Gerdt).[21] Consequently, when the work was given in a concert performance (with costumes, incidentally, that were many and various), the hero was simply left out, an omission that only benefited the ensemble. I shall therefore refer to the adagio as a pas de cinq.

It is common knowledge that it is extremely difficult to construct a harmonious choreographic composition with one male dancer and four females. No Soviet ballet master has ever succeeded in doing so. There is a well-conceived pas de six for three men and three women (in other words, an equal number of men and women) in Act II of Vakhtang Chabukiani's *Laurencia*,[22] and I consider my own composition for two women and four men in the last act of *The Bright Stream* a success. But no one except Petipa ever took the risk of staging a pas de cinq with one man and four women. What a perfect grasp of the forms of classical dance Petipa must have had in order to be capable of creating such a piece! As far as harmonious choreographic construction and the sequence and placement of movements are concerned, it is so faultless that it cannot be equaled. Even Fokine acknowledged this (he gave an outstanding performance of the male role in the ensemble, devising his own Egyptian-style arm positions). The pas de cinq in *The Daughter of Pharaoh* is an unsurpassed masterpiece of choreographic sonata form. What makes this all the more important is the fact that the sonata form is absent from Pugni's music.

The pas de cinq began with small group poses in which all the performers participated. An adagio for one man and four women could not be anything but unusual. It was not constructed in the same way as other grand adagios, using a variety of supports; rather, it developed through distinctive figurations, moving from one group pose to another.

I am convinced that Petipa was inspired to stage this work by Fedor Tolstoy's sketches for the ballet *The Aeolian Harp*. These sketches are reproduced in Yury Slonimsky's book on Charles-Louis Didelot,[23] and I am sure that Petipa must have seen them. Of course, Petipa did not copy the poses from Tolstoy's drawings, but their structure was the starting point from which his choreography evolved.

The opening, which was based on group poses, turned into a section of dance; then followed the development, variations, and a concluding coda.

I have referred to variations, but a glance at the piano score reveals that these variations are not musically distinct. They do not exist except as part of the whole: the music of each variation flows from that of the previous one. (Incidentally, this is the only music in the whole ballet that merits attention.) In the dance variations, solo performances predominated, but occasionally characters came together and danced in pairs, either two women or one woman and the man.

It is impossible to describe all the movements and their sequence without actually watching a performance, so I shall confine myself to naming the main ones, including the linking glissades, pas de bourrées, and coupés that usually serve as preparation for the step to follow. These steps included gliding movements in a fluid arabesque, or turning on the spot, also emboîté turns, grands sauts de basque, grandes cabrioles with the body thrown backward in midair, and, frequently, cabrioles en croisé, which are very difficult to perform. The beginning of the man's variation, with its écarté pose, was very original and not what would normally be expected in a male dance. Overall, the movements were not just set to fill up the music; instead, they were arranged so that one movement gave rise to the next. This meant that a movement could serve as a preparation for the next movement yet at the same time play an essential part in the process of the choreographic development. In other words, nothing in this large-scale classical work was present merely "by chance" or for the sole purpose of providing a metrical match for the music. Everything had a function and flowed from the development and counterbalance of the themes. To put the point in a different way (if we can speak of choreography in these terms), the dance tonality in this work was not accidental but determined by the development of choreographic themes. As a consequence, the work was easily accessible even to nonspecialists.

Only in one section of the pas de cinq—the heroine Aspicia's variation—did Petipa fail to live up to his usual high standard. This variation, which was not connected in any way with the choreography of the rest of the piece, was created for Kchessinska. The pseudo-Iranian movements were performed with the help of a dagger and a shawl, creating an effect that was completely out of keeping both with the ancient Egyptian setting and with the purely classical form of the pas de cinq as a whole. Even the dancer's headdress—no doubt by Fabergé—bore scant resemblance to the Egyptian style. This variation stood out in stark contrast to the rest of the ensemble because it was superfluous and false.

I have no doubt that the variation was staged because of pressure from the all-powerful Kchessinska. Her particular fondness for this nonsensical ballet is perfectly understandable: it gave her the opportunity to play the part of a royal personage! We can see why, on her retirement, Kchessinska asked Vladimir Telyakovsky, the director of the Imperial Theaters, to keep the part of the Pharaoh's daughter for her alone and not to give it to other ballerinas.

Fortunately, this styleless variation did not ruin the rest of the pas de cinq. The dances of the other characters, including the male dancer's variation and the coda in which all took part, were enough to obliterate the heroine's anti-artistic blunderings, and the public, which did not understand the subtleties of the choreographic composition of this work, greeted all the dancers, even those whose performances were not particularly impressive, with ecstatic applause. This surely indicates that the public appreciated the work as a whole.

I have already suggested a link between Petipa and Didelot, of whom, according to Slonimsky, Fedor Tolstoy was a student. I am equally convinced that Fokine's work is a continuation of this link. The direct influence of the pas de cinq manifests itself in ballets such as *Eros, Les Sylphides,* and *Papillons*,[24] in the asymmetry of the groupings (this is especially true of *Papillons,* a ballet now completely forgotten).

Nowadays we can only regret the loss of this masterpiece, which was a steppingstone to modern choreography. I have described it not for the purpose of restoration, which in any case would be an impossible task, but in order to convey at least an impression of it to contemporary choreographers. I consider it very important to do so: there is profound inner substance to the composition of this and similar masterpieces, such as we find in music. Until recently, our choreographers and dance specialists have generally overlooked this fact; if they have mentioned it at all, they have done so only in half-syllables, as if they doubted it. But, as far as I am concerned, it is precisely this richness of exclusively choreographic content that renders the art of ballet equal to that of music.

To return once more to Petipa, there is no shortage of instances where this great master has been underrated, both in his own time and in the present day. For example, certain idle faultfinders have accused Petipa of "standing in the way of Lev Ivanov." This is completely untrue. If it were true, Petipa would never have allowed Ivanov to stage the white acts of *Swan Lake, The Polovtsian Dances* in *Prince Igor* (in which, incidentally, I danced the part of one of the Polovtsian boys),

the Hungarian Rhapsody to music by Liszt that was incorporated into Alexander Gorsky's production of *The Little Humpbacked Horse,* or ballets such as *The Nutcracker, The Enchanted
Forest, The Haarlem Tulip, The Awakening of Flora,* and *The
Mikado's Daughter,* among others.[25] In fact the evidence suggests the reverse: that Petipa greatly respected Ivanov, and,
indeed, Gerdt, Legat, Shiryaev, and many others have actually
assured me that this was the case. Rumors of Petipa's unfriend-
liness toward Ivanov have been put about by those who were
or are hostile to and envious of both Petipa and Ivanov, but I
am prepared to defend a great master against mere apprentices.
Alas, there have always been far fewer masters than apprentices,
the latter being less interested in creative work than in self-
advertisement. (This, incidentally, is a point that applies to
other spheres of activity besides choreography.)

If this great master were still alive, I would advise him to
change his name from "Petipa" to "Grandpa," which would be
far more appropriate.[b]

b. This is a play on the French words "petit" meaning "small" and "grand"
meaning "great."

The Choreography of the Shades
Scene in *La Bayadère*

I have asked a number of people who have seen "The Kingdom of the Shades" from *La Bayadère*—people of differing levels of education and intellect and from a variety of social backgrounds—whether they liked the work, and, if so, why. They all answered in the affirmative: they liked it; some of them liked it very much. But only a few of them could say why, and even those who could were not always very precise as to their reasons. Then I asked them a different question: whether they liked Beethoven. Again, the answer was "yes," and again no one (with the exception of music specialists) could explain why, and this despite the fact that a great deal has been written about Beethoven, whereas nothing has been written—not even by ballet critics such as Akim Volynsky and Valerian Svetlov[1]— about "The Kingdom of the Shades," apart from some superficial notices concerning particular performers. Choreographers generally made reference to the existence of some excellent and worthwhile arabesques, développés à la seconde, ports de bras, jetés, tours, chaînés, and so on in the Shades scene, but they could not say why these movements were so pleasing here, when in other works the same movements failed to produce the same effect. It goes without saying that superficial answers of this nature will never satisfy anyone who sees choreography as a great art.

I asked myself the same question, and I attempted to answer it without resorting to a mere list of movements. What is the reason that everyone likes this particular piece of choreography?

Is it because of its Indian exotica? But neither the poses nor the movements in the scene are visibly Indian; they contain nothing of the everyday India that we all know. However, the spiritual aspect of the scene is a different matter. Consider, for example, how the Indians stand with their palms together in front of the chest, a pose that they adopt in circumstances such as meeting people or conversing. It is a pose full of good will, respect, and deference to the other person, without any hint of slavish submissiveness. It reflects the Indian perception of the ideal human relationship. This is what we see in Petipa's "The Kingdom of the Shades," though he does not reproduce everyday Indian poses but rather creates choreographic positions that accord with them in terms of mood. The presence of this "spiritual" India in "The Kingdom of the Shades" makes itself felt from the moment the performers enter for the very first time. There are good reasons for characterizing the dancers as "Shades." A man's shade or shadow reproduces his every movement in the finest detail and thereby reveals his spiritual self, but it does not have the same reality as his material form. Petipa's ballet conveys a generalized impression of "Shades," but in the abstract; anything more concrete would invariably lead to naturalism, which has always been the enemy of true realism in ballet.[2] People watching the Shades scene perceive its essence in the same way that they experience strong emotions when they listen to a piece of music such as Beethoven's "Appassionata."[3] Each individual finds something in "The Kingdom of the Shades" that corresponds to something within himself, something that is awakened by the choreography of the work, just as anyone who listens to music hears it in his own particular way. One must search the depths of one's imagination for a personal reaction to "The Kingdom of the Shades." The scene evokes a spiritual response that is as hard to explain in words as the impression created by a piece of music.

"The Kingdom of the Shades" shows evidence of great skill in realistic choreography. This is choreography of the highest order; its richness is obvious and quite independent of auxiliary elements such as narrative content, pantomime, or theatrical props. To my mind, not even Lev Ivanov's beautiful swans or Fokine's sylphs can compare with the Shades in this respect.

In all that has been written about "The Kingdom of the Shades," no mention has ever been made of the one major factor that differentiates this work from countless others that are superficially eye-catching but lack a profound inner substance. In the principles of its composition, "The Kingdom of the Shades" bears a strong resemblance to the musical sonata allegro. The sonata form in music, with its exposition, elaboration, and reprise of themes (or opening, development, and dénouement) is rich and profound, for the most part independent of any narrative content. The choreography of "The Kingdom of the Shades" develops in exactly the same way, but, unfortunately, dance specialists have failed to notice the fact; certainly, I have never found a single reference to it in any existing publication.

"The Kingdom of the Shades" contains all the typical features of the sonata form. It is possible to identify an exposition, elaboration, and dénouement in the treatment of certain choreographic themes. The interaction of these themes forms the basis of the scene, the emphasis of which is more on broad meaning than on narrative content. There is one proviso: although choreographic sonata form is similar to musical sonata form, the two are not identical. In the case of music, the "raw material" is sound, whereas, in the case of choreography, it is movement; the former is perceived aurally, the latter visually. The difference is significant.

As in any musical work in sonata form, a choreographic piece in this form should contain alongside the main theme various secondary themes that develop in parallel to the main theme and are contrapuntal to it. In the second section—the development—these themes may be "in different keys," to use musical terminology. In choreographic terms, this means that they may reappear in different alignments or be made more complex by the introduction of new choreographic themes that flow out of the original ones or arise from within them. For example, a simple assemblé without elevation may acquire elevation, possibly changing from a petit assemblé to a grand assemblé and even into an assemblé en tournant; that is to say, it may become more elaborate through the addition of midair turns, possibly in various alignments—effacé, croisé, with the back, face, or side toward the front of the stage. In compositions based upon variations, these themes in the second (development) section may be refined virtuoso pieces; they may interact with new secondary themes to reappear side by side in the reprise. The coda is essential in a choreographic work in sonata form. Some codas consist of a set of impressive movements chosen at random (an example is the last act of *Don Quixote*),[4] but a choreographic coda should be a dénouement of precisely the sort we find in "The Kingdom of the Shades," where a crescendo of virtuosity is justified by the choreographic development, rather than being a mere concoction of random movements.

The first part of "The Kingdom of the Shades"—the exposition—is the entrée and waltz, which may also be broken down into sections. The very beginning of the entrée consists of a simple pair of walking steps and an arabesque in plié. The plié is very small and transient. The foot is then placed on the floor to the rear, while the body bends backward with the arms overhead in third position.[5] These movements—the steps, the arabesque, and the backward bend of the body as the dancer winds across the stage—continue for some time. But one is not aware of the duration of the dance, just as one is not aware of the apparent monotony of Ravel's *Bolero*,[6] where the same theme is repeated over and over again. On the contrary, this motion is a source of aesthetic pleasure: as the number of participants in the scene grows, so the tension increases.

Now for the second section of the entrée. The forward motion and the arabesque lead into a slow développé à la seconde. This pose is related to the arabesque in that the leg is stretched out to nearly the same extent, but to the side rather than to the rear; also, the arabesque is performed on pointe.[7] Next come slow, backward-moving pas de bourrée,[8] traveling steps as before but this time performed with a classical refinement: the feet are on pointe instead of being flat on the ground.

This is the second rise to pointe. Whereas in the first part of the entrée the arabesque was effacé, subsequently it recurs in various alignments and forms. Remember that the arabesque effacé is one of the most still poses in choreography. But an arabesque croisé, in which the legs cross, is not at all still, for it is easy to make the transition from the arabesque croisé to any movement with a turn, and a turn is the beginning of a pirouette, a movement that, be it fast or slow, is brimming with energy.[9]

The reverse pas de bourrée on pointe give way to the backward bend of the body we saw at the outset, but again there is a crescendo: the dancers do not simply bend their bodies back with their arms in third position but drop onto one knee on the ground while the other leg is thrust forward in a tendu.

This is the end of the first part of the exposition and the beginning of the transition to the second part, the waltz, in which the movements presented earlier become modified. The soloists appear. They perform the same movements as the corps de ballet positioned along the sides, but the figure is different because there are only three soloists. Both the corps de ballet and the soloists execute an increasing number of movements on pointe, and instances where the feet are flat on the ground become less and less frequent.

As this part of the exposition is a waltz, there is no need for me to name all the interim movements. Here they function as preparation,[a] links to the ballonné in various alignments and to the à la seconde. It is much more difficult to perform these movements to the tempo of a waltz than it is to a slow tempo, because the à la seconde is a long, drawn-out movement and more appropriate to an adagio. Where the tempo is fast, it is necessary to "throw" the leg up into the extension, and at maximum height, as well. Among the new movements in the second part of the exposition—the waltz—we find petites sissonnes and ballonnés;[10] the écarté alignment changes because it is executed to a fast tempo instead of to a slow adagio.

a. That is to say, preparation for a movement. If the preparation is itself a movement, then it too requires preparation.

The waltz is followed by the adagio of Nikiya and Solor, where the ballerina, supported by her partner, performs a saut de basque, a développé into écarté à la seconde followed by a turn into arabesque. These gently flowing movements (apart from the saut de basque, which has already appeared in the ensemble's dance) form the basis of the soloists' adagio. Then, with a series of jetés, one after the other, the ballerina disappears into the wings,[11] while her partner follows slowly behind her.

In the last part of the exposition, the soloists establish the choreographic theme, and the corps de ballet repeats it. Here the main additional movements are port de bras. The ports de bras—dances of the arms—provide a marvelous resolution for the final part of the exposition. The movements introduced by the soloists—first, the port de bras, then a series of jetés[12]—are immediately taken up and repeated by the entire corps de ballet. In the finale of the exposition, every member of the corps de ballet lies on the ground shielded by one arm while continuing to perform the port de bras with the other.[13] This creates such a powerful and poetic effect that it all but effaces the female soloist, even though she herself is performing truly virtuosic movements: gentle battements à la seconde and in attitude, sophisticated turns on the spot, double turns culminating in the arabesques and attitudes seen earlier, and so on. It is in the ports de bras that we pick up an echo of the dances of India:[14] the use of the arms is characteristic of Indian dance, as it is of dances of the peoples of the Middle East. European choreographers undoubtedly borrowed movement ideas from the East and reworked them in the classical spirit. Petipa's introduction of these ports de bras into the dances of the Shades was a stroke of genius that many dance specialists simply ignored.

The ballerina in "The Kingdom of the Shades" is not the same Nikiya who appears in the other scenes of *La Bayadère*. In the Shades scene, we lose sight of Nikiya the Hindu dancing girl; we forget her, because the scene is about much more than the experiences of a single individual. When the port de bras is brought into the adagio by the ballerina and immediately taken up by the corps de ballet, the result is something in the manner of a two-part choreographic canon in which the choreographic leader is the solo dancer Nikiya and the choreographic community is the corps de ballet. (There is no doubt that Petipa was well educated in music: his use of the sonata form in "The Kingdom of the Shades" and of other choreographic forms, such as the choreographic canon mentioned here, is evidence of the fact.) As a choreographer, I am naturally used to seeing various ports de bras, but these never fail to charm me, and I marvel at Petipa's skill.

The development section of "The Kingdom of the Shades" is in the form of variations, of which there are four. These variations consist predominantly of the movements upon which the exposition is based. However, certain new elements arising out of or related to the movements of the opening section are introduced in each variation, and the movements as they occur in the variations are noticeably more sophisticated and complex. For example, in the exposition, there are many instances where the foot is placed flat on the ground, but in the variations, such instances occur only when a dancer is running across the stage.

Because many dancers are unaware of the significance of the run as a link between the different parts of a variation, they perform it as if it were somehow detached from the rest of the piece. (I shall discuss this point in detail in my article "The Role of the Male Dancer.") The walk or run in *La Bayadère,* for example, should be classical; it should not be deliberately made "original," the special creation of a particular artist. Many soloists change the run because they have not grasped the essence of "The Kingdom of the Shades." The point here is that the corps de ballet has a function that is no less important than that of the soloists; therefore, if soloists place themselves at the fore, the perfect construction of the scene is shattered.

In the following analysis of the individual variations, my purpose is not to describe the sequence of movements and to explain how they should be performed for the benefit of the rehearsal director. My purpose is to uncover the underlying idea of Petipa's work and to make it comprehensible. What I have to say will be of only minor assistance to the rehearsal director.

In the first variation, which is essentially a little scherzino, there are many movements that have already appeared fleetingly in the exposition. Among the new movements in the second part of the variation, there is a jeté pas de chat with a turn following in attitude on pointe; this is repeated three times in succession. After a run linking the second part of the variation to the third, there is a relatively new, elaborate movement that completes the variation. It consists of a plié and a sissonne into arabesque on pointe with a powerful forward motion; this progressive movement is repeated several times. As she moves down the diagonal, lowering and raising her body, the dancer appears to be floating. This movement is reminiscent of the first entry of the corps de ballet in the exposition section, but it is more complicated, both because of the increased speed and because the dancer is on pointe.

Although the first variation is a choreographic scherzino, its character is lyrical-romantic. The scherzino form is the equivalent of a smile, not of laughter. This variation should be performed not by terre-à-terre dancers—they are best suited to the role of comic ingenue—but by one whose forte is the lyrical-romantic.

I have said that "The Kingdom of the Shades" is lyrical-romantic in character. The second variation has a hint of the lyrical-heroic that makes itself felt right at the start of the variation. It also contains some new choreographic themes. The first section of the variation is constructed around a grande cabriole down the diagonal, which is repeated four times. Then the dancer runs back to the position on the stage from which she began the variation and performs all the movements down the diagonal a second time. In the second section, there are four ordinary waltz balancés with two stops in arabesque, one to each side.[15] Both the waltz and the arabesque have already appeared in the exposition. The third section is a sort of echo of the third section of the first variation, with the plié and relevé in an arabesque, but the legs are different, the position is now attitude en avant, and the heroic coloring is retained. At the end, the cabrioles are repeated twice, and the variation finishes with a saut de basque and chaîné turns. It will be remembered that a supported demi-saut de basque followed by a pose in écarté à la seconde was introduced in the first soloist's adagio. Here the movement is performed without the support of the male partner, which means that it becomes more difficult and at the same time takes on a heroic tinge. Vaganova danced this variation well, but she was surpassed by Marina Semenova,[16] whom I cast in *La Bayadère* when she was still a pupil at school.

As the third variation develops, it reveals a deep lyricism. It does not contain any new movements apart from a petite sissonne.[17] It consists, for the most part, of variations of movements from the exposition, but in different alignments. Here we find the same à la seconde extensions and the same arabesque, but with an intervening sissonne that we have also seen before. The variation ends with a headlong run on pointe down the diagonal, coming to a sudden standstill. In the first variation, the danseuse appeared to be floating; in this one, she moves along the same diagonal, but, as she runs, she seems lifted above the ground, like an apparition or a shadow. This run, an apparently simple movement, is in fact very difficult to perform in the manner required. For example, a terre-à-terre dancer will be unable to convey the right impression: she will execute the run "on little hooves" (to use Volynsky's words); she will not be "released from" or "above" the ground, although this sense of release is essential. The variation ends with a grand pas de chat.

The fourth variation is the most important, not because it is performed by the ballerina (Nikiya) but because the second part of the work ends with it. It is, as it were, the culmination of the development stage. The variation begins with turns—demi-tours in attitude. Nowadays, ballerinas attempt to execute a full attitude turn, as if to defy us with their technique.[18] Petipa, however, did not stipulate a full turn, only a demi-tour, or half-turn, a slower, more floating, "fluid" movement. The descent from pointe to the sole of the foot and the immediate rise back to pointe for the next demi-tour is performed as if it were a single continuous movement. According to Petipa's conception, the subsequent repetitions of these relevés should not be uniform (that is to say, equal to a demi-tour) but may be performed in the space of a demi-tour or a third or a quarter of a tour, thus retaining their fluid quality. Petipa's achievement is truly brilliant, for, in fact, turns are not fundamentally continuous. The rotation gives the outward appearance of continuity, but the appearance is false, even when there are a large number of pirouettes (between sixteen and twenty turns, as performed by Moscow artists such as Vasily Tikhomirov, Alexandre Volinine, and Fedor Kozlov,[19] among others). Petipa reinforced the impression created by the slow demi-tours by placing in the ballerina's hands a piece of tulle that would fly upward at the end of the first part of the variation. By attempting to execute a whole turn in attitude, ballerinas inflict severe damage upon Petipa's whole design. A full turn cannot convey a sense of calm, and it interferes with the lyrical-romantic tone of the work. However, it is more difficult for the ballerina to perform a half-turn in attitude than it is to perform a full turn. The reason for this is that a turn generates centrifugal force, as a result of which the movement continues on its own momentum. This momentum prevents the ballerina from performing the turn as smoothly as it should be performed in this part of the variation. Thus, those artists who attempt a full turn at this point are tacitly acknowledging that dance cantilena à la Taglioni is beyond them.

At this point, it is useful for the purpose of comparison to remember Geba Kanovy. One cannot imagine her making a jerky movement or turn when coming out of a position. Geba Kanovy does not walk, she "floats" through the air! The demi-tours in attitude that Petipa uses in this variation make us acutely aware of the peculiarly fluid nature of the movement.

The second part of the variation is based on the jeté that first appeared in the exposition.[20] Here the jeté is performed in a different alignment, toward the back of the stage. After the jeté, there follows by way of preparation a pas de bourrée on pointe and a double tour en dehors that again comes to a halt in an arabesque, but with the ballerina facing the audience. Here we see a further development of the arabesque, which is one of the work's main positions. The choreographic phrase is repeated twice in succession, and then comes the transition to the third part of the variation—again a walk/run. Pavlova was the only ballerina to preserve the character of the variation when performing this run; all the others apparently regard the run as a chance for them to have a rest, and so the variation's line of development is lost.

The third part of the variation consists of a walk on pointe, a pas de bourrée that comes to a halt on one supporting leg, then on the other.[21] This is a progressive movement. It is repeated twice, after which the variation finishes like the third variation: there is a forceful pas de bourrée with open arms, not this time down the diagonal but toward the front of the stage, and the ballerina comes to an unexpected halt, not with a pas de chat but in an attitude. This stop on one foot actually creates the impression that the run continues; similarly, when performed by Geba Kanovy, the pose made us believe that she was moving through clouds.

All the choreographic themes I have described reappear in the final section of the work, the reprise/dénouement. Here they are further developed in opposition to each other. As the themes develop, they are performed alternately by the soloists and the corps de ballet. The effect is of many people running, an effect that is amplified by the fact that there are always new dancers at the front. Both the soloists and the corps de ballet reach a climax. That of the corps de ballet—the episode where the dancers "skip" backward in an arabesque, almost floating— is no less impressive than that of the soloists.

I should mention that in this scene from *La Bayadère*, as in Petipa's other ballets, unacceptable changes are sometimes made. Because they do not grasp the essence of the work, dancers performing the role of Solor replace the cabriole and the saut de basque in the coda with movements they are better able to perform, their main concern being their own perceived success and not the meaning of the work as a whole. They often justify their action by pointing out that Pavel Gerdt omitted the male coda when he danced the role of Solor. However, Gerdt gave up performing the cabriole and the saut de basque in the coda because of age and with Petipa's permission. When he was younger, he performed all the movements and never replaced them with others that were his own particular favorites. He did what the dénouement of this work demanded, as it was set by Petipa. I talked to Gerdt, and he confirmed that the danseur's coda was based on the musical repetition of Nikiya's coda and that the movements consisted of a cabriole derrière preceded by a tombé (preceded directly by a tombé, without a step before the cabriole), followed by a step forward into an arabesque. In the course of the cabriole, the dancer would move forward, and the greater his progress, the more beautiful the appearance of the movement. This combination would be performed twice, followed by an entrechat-six. The whole sequence would be repeated using the other leg. Then came sauts de basque in a circle, as performed earlier by Nikiya. The impression created was of a dialogue between the two soloists, or, more accurately, of an animated choreographic exchange between themes incarnated by the soloists.

It is also annoying when male dancers perform not the classical jeté en tournant, to which I would have no objection, but the kind of split-leg jump usually seen in folk dance ensembles. This vulgarizes the finale of "The Kingdom of the Shades." Remember that a true jeté en tournant always ends with a beautiful attitude—the god Mercury's pose![22] If the jeté en tournant is executed in a circle with the right leg to the right, then the left leg is in an attitude, while the left arm is raised in a semicircle so that the hand ends up positioned over the left eye. This is a strictly classical pose and has nothing in common with crude split-leg jumps.

Petipa's "Kingdom of the Shades" ends with the members of the corps de ballet in poses from the adagio in the exposition section: the choreographer has them on the floor and repeating the port de bras with one arm while they lift themselves very slightly off the ground with the other. This conveys the impression of an action that is not as yet completed. At the same time, the soloists repeat the basic pose: Solor supports Nikiya, who stands in an attitude.

In my description, I have tried to highlight the fact that this brilliant piece of choreography is not merely a collection of movements that happen to work well but a work inspired by a single grand idea. Hence its structure, which I consider to be that of a choreographic sonata form. "The Kingdom of the Shades" in *La Bayadère* is a great work of choreography in which themes are elaborated and brought into confrontation with each other so that new themes are generated. I am well aware that this work is open to even deeper interpretation; it is possible that I have missed something vital. However, this is the first time that an analysis of this sort has been attempted.

The following is a list of the main works by Fedor Lopukhov, ballets created solely by the choreographer and in collaboration with others and his productions of works by other choreographers. The main source is Lopukhov's own chronology in his *Sixty Years in Ballet* (348–352), supplemented by information from Galina Dobrovolskaya's list in *Fedor Lopukhov* (312–315) and the Soviet *Ballet Encyclopedia*. Reference has also been made to the *International Dictionary of Ballet*, Natalia Roslavleva's *Era of the Russian Ballet*, Elizabeth Souritz's *Soviet Choreographers in the 1920s*, and Mary Grace Swift's *The Art of the Dance in the USSR*. Where disagreement exists among the sources, I have followed the Soviet *Ballet Encyclopedia*.

The name of the librettist is given when this is neither Lopukhov himself nor the composer. GATOB is the acronym for the Petrograd (from 1924 Leningrad) State Academic Theater of Opera and Ballet, later known as the Kirov Theater and today by its prerevolutionary name, the Maryinsky Theater.

ORIGINAL BALLETS

The Mexican Saloon
Music: Leonid Goncharov
Premiere: Petrograd, Theater of Musical Drama, 1916
Note: The 1916 date is Lopukhov's. In *The History of the Ballet Section of the Petersburg Theater School*, Mikhail Borisoglebsky includes *The Mexican Saloon* in the list of ballets performed on the St. Petersburg stage, giving the premiere as 30 March 1918 in the Bolshoi Zal of the Conservatory, but in the article on Lopukhov he says that the work was performed in

1916 at the Comedy Theater. The *Theater Review* for 1916 makes no mention of the ballet in relation to either this venue or the Theater of Musical Drama.

The Dream
Music: Nikolai Shcherbachev
Premiere: Petrograd, Theater of Musical Drama, 1916
Note: Again, the 1916 date is Lopukhov's. Borisoglebsky (in the above-mentioned volume) lists the premiere as 30 March 1918 at the Theater of Musical Drama, but the press does not support this. According to the *Theater Review*, the Moscow dancers Alexandra Balashova and Leonid Zhukov were appearing at the Theater of Musical Drama on that date.

Firebird
Music: Igor Stravinsky
Design: Alexander Golovin
Premiere: Petrograd, GATOB, 2 October 1921

Dance Symphony
Music: Ludwig van Beethoven
Design: Pavel Goncharov
Premiere: Petrograd, GATOB, 7 March 1923

Night on Bald Mountain
Music: Modest Mussorgsky, arr. Nikolai Rimsky-Korsakov
Sets: Konstantin Korovin (from the ballet *Mlada*)
Costumes: Makari Domrachev
Premiere: Leningrad, GATOB, 26 March 1924

The Red Whirlwind
Music: Vladimir Deshevov
Design: Leonid Chupiatov
Premiere: Leningrad, GATOB, 29 October 1924

Pulcinella
Music: Igor Stravinsky

Design: Vladimir Dimitriev
Premiere: Leningrad, GATOB, 16 May 1926

Renard
Music: Igor Stravinsky
Design: Vladimir Dimitriev
Premiere: Leningrad, GATOB, 2 January 1927

The Ice Maiden
Music: Edvard Grieg, arr. Boris Asafiev
Design: Alexander Golovin
Premiere: Leningrad, GATOB, 27 April 1927

The Serf Ballerina
Music: Klimenti Korchmarev
Design: V. A. Shuko
Premiere: Leningrad, GATOB, 11 December 1927

The Red Poppy
Libretto: Mikhail Kurilko, rev. Fedor Lopukov
Music: Reinhold Glière
Design: Boris Erbstein
Premiere: Leningrad, GATOB, 20 January 1929
Note: Act I was choreographed by Lopukhov, Acts II and II
by Vladimir Ponomarev and Leonid Leontiev, respectively. The
overall production was supervised by Lopukhov.

The Nutcracker
Music: Pyotr Tchaikovsky
Design: Vladimir Dimitriev
Premiere: Leningrad, GATOB, 27 October 1929

Bolt
Music: Dmitri Shostakovich
Design: Tatiana Bruni, Georgy Korshikov
Premiere: Leningrad, GATOB, 8 April 1931

Harlequinade
Music: Riccardo Drigo
Design: Mikhail Bobyshov
Premiere: Leningrad, Maly Theater, 6 June 1933

Coppélia
Music: Léo Delibes
Design: Mikhail Bobyshov
Premiere: Leningrad, Maly Theater, 4 April 1934

The Bright Stream
Libretto: Fedor Lopukhov, Adrian Piotrovsky
Music: Dmitri Shostakovich
Premiere: Leningrad, Maly Theater, 4 April 1935

Christmas Eve
Libretto: Yuri Slonimsky
Music: Boris Asafiev
Design: A. A. Kolomoitsev
Premiere: Leningrad, Kirov Theater (by students of the Choreographic School), 15 June 1938
Note: Act II was choreographed by Lopukhov, Act I by Vladimir Bourmeister.

The Nightingale
Libretto: Yuri Slonimsky, Alexei Ermolaev
Music: Mikhail Kroshner
Design: B. A. Matrunin
Premiere: Minsk Opera and Ballet Theater, 5 November 1939
Note: Lopukhov choreographed this ballet with Alexei Ermolaev.

Taras Bulba
Libretto: Semyon Kaplan
Music: Vasily Soloviev-Sedoy
Design: Vadim Ryndin
Premiere: Leningrad, Kirov Ballet, 12 December 1940

Akbilyak
Libretto: V. Smirnov and M. Tursunov
Music: Sergei Vasilenko
Design: Meli Musaev
Premiere: Tashkent, Navoi Theater, 7 November 1943
Note: The Uzbek dances were choreographed by Mukka-ram Turgunbaeva. Usta Alim Kamilov served as production consultant.

La Fille Mal Gardée
Music: Peter Hertel
Premiere: Chkalovo (Orenburg), Maly Theater, 1 May 1944
Note: During World War II, the Maly troupe temporarily relocated to Chkalovo. In 1947, Lopukhov staged the ballet at the Ukrainian Theater of Opera and Ballet in Kiev.

Spring Fairy Tale
Libretto: Yuri Slonimsky
Music: Boris Asafiev (based on Tchaikovsky)
Design: Simon Virsaladze
Premiere: Leningrad, Kirov Ballet, 8 January 1947

Love Ballad
Music: Pyotr Tchaikovsky (excerpts from *The Seasons*)
Premiere: Leningrad, Maly Ballet, 26 March 1959

Pictures at an Exhibition
Music: Modest Mussorgsky
Design: Alexander Lushin
Premiere: Moscow, Stanislavsky and Nemirovich-Danchenko Theater, 5 September 1963

PRODUCTIONS OF BALLETS BY OTHER CHOREOGRAPHERS

The Sleeping Beauty
Music: Pyotr Tchaikovsky
Choreography: Marius Petipa

Design: Konstantin Korovin, P. R. Ovchinnikov, V. S. Iakov-
lev, S. I. Petrov, N. A. Klodt
Premiere: Petrograd, GATOB, 8 October 1922

Harlequinade
Music: Riccardo Drigo
Choreography: Marius Petipa
Premiere: Petrograd, GATOB, 25 October 1922

Raymonda
Music: Alexander Glazunov
Choreography: Marius Petipa
Premiere: Petrograd, GATOB, 29 October 1922

The Little Humpbacked Horse
Music: Cesare Pugni
Choreography: Marius Petipa
Premiere: Petrograd, GATOB, 19 November 1922

The Nutcracker
Music: Pyotr Tchaikovsky
Choreography: Lev Ivanov
Premiere: Petrograd, GATOB, 4 February 1923
Note: This was staged by Lopukhov with Alexander Shiriaev.

Eros
Music: Pyotr Tchaikovsky
Choreography: Michel Fokine
Design: Mikhail Bobyshov
Premiere: Petrograd, GATOB, 6 May 1923

Egyptian Nights
Music: Anton Arensky
Choreography: Michel Fokine
Sets: Orest Allegri
Costumes: M. P. Zandin

Premiere: Petrograd, GATOB, 6 May 1923
Note: This was staged by Lopukhov and Alexander Chekrygin, after Fokine.

Le Pavillon d'Armide
Music: Nicholas Tcherepnine
Choreography: Michel Fokine
Design: Alexandre Benois
Premiere: Petrograd, GATOB, 6 May 1923
Note: This was staged by Lopukhov and Alexander Chekrygin, after Fokine.

Don Quixote
Music: Ludwig Minkus
Choreography: Alexander Gorsky
Design: Alexander Golovin, Konstantin Korovin
Premiere: Petrograd, GATOB, 30 September 1923
Note: This was staged by Lopukhov, after Gorsky.

Swan Lake
Music: Pyotr Tchaikovsky
Choreography: Marius Petipa, Lev Ivanov
Sets: Boris Volkov
Costumes: Tatiana Bruni
Premiere: 22 June 1945
Note: In 1948, Lopukhov mounted the ballet at the Lithuanian Theater of Opera and Ballet in Vilnius.

Swan Lake
Music: Pyotr Tchaikovsky
Choreography: Marius Petipa, Lev Ivanov
Premiere: Leningrad, Maly Theater, 19 July 1958
Note: This production, which Lopukhov staged with Konstantin Boyarksy, was a reconstruction of the original Petipa/Ivanov choreography. In 1958, Lopukhov staged a revival of the ballet at the Ukrainian Theater of Opera and Ballet in Kiev.

La Bayadère (The Shades Scene)
Music: Ludwig Minkus
Choreography: Marius Petipa
Premiere: Moscow, Bolshoi Ballet, 1962
Note: This production is listed by Lopukhov in *Sixty Years in Ballet.*

Egyptian Nights
Music: Anton Arensky
Choreography: Michel Fokine
Sets: N. Z. Melnikov
Costumes: N. A. Tikhonova
Premiere: Leningrad, Kirov Theater, 15 December 1962
Note: This was a revival of the 1923 production staged by Lopukhov and Alexander Chekrygin, after Fokine.

Notes

INTRODUCTION

1. The main references in English to *The Ballet Master and His Art* are Elizabeth Souritz, *Soviet Choreographers in the 1920s,* trans. Lynn Visson, ed. with additional trans. Sally Banes (Durham: Duke University Press, 1990), 275; and Natalia Roslavleva, *Era of the Russian Ballet 1770–1965* (London: Gollancz, 1966), 203–205. A key source in Russian is Galina Dobrovolskaya, *Fedor Lopukhov* (Moscow–Leningrad: Iskusstvo, 1976), chap. 4. Note that the title of Lopukhov's treatise has usually been rendered in English as "Ways of a Ballet Master" or "Paths of a Ballet Master." We have opted for a less literal translation from the Russian but one that we feel conveys the spirit of Lopukhov's intentions.

2. The name Petrograd was used until 1924, after which date the city was called Leningrad. In the text, it is referred to by its name at the time in question.

3. For an introduction to *Dance Symphony* and its performance history, the most important writing in English to date is Souritz, *Soviet Choreographers,* 266–277.

4. Fedor Lupokhov, "The Choreography of the Shades Scene in *La Bayadère*" and "Petipa as Creator of the Choreographic Sonata Form," in *Choreographic Revelations* (Khoreograficheskie otkrovennosti) (Moscow: Iskusstvo, 1972), 57–65, 69–79.

5. Fedor Lopukhov, *Sixty Years in Ballet* (Shestdesiat let v balete) (Moscow: Iskusstvo, 1966), 243. In fact, Lopukhov's first choreography dates from 1906.

6. Ibid., 213.

7. Lopukhov came from a theatrical family, the eldest of four who trained in ballet at the St. Petersburg Theater School. His sister Lydia Lopokova became a star of the Diaghilev Ballets Russes and later played an important role in the development of British ballet.

8. Mary Grace Swift, *The Art of the Dance in the USSR* (Notre Dame, Ind.: University of Notre Dame Press, 1968), 37.

9. Gleb Struve, "The Transition from Russian to Soviet Literature," in *Literature and Revolution in Soviet Russia 1917–1962,* ed. Max Hayward and Leopold Labedz (Westport, Conn.: Greenwood Press, 1963), 24.

10. Swift, *Art of the Dance,* 89–91.

11. Ibid., 103–112.

12. Sally Banes, "Introduction and Context to Soviet Ballet in the 1920s," in Souritz, *Soviet Choreographers*, 6.

13. Lopukhov, *Sixty Years*, 163.

14. Georgii Kovalenko, "The Constructivist Stage," in *Theatre in Revolution: Russian Avant-Garde Stage Design 1913–1935*, ed. Nancy van Norman Baer (London: Thames and Hudson, 1991), 178.

15. Souritz, *Soviet Choreographers*, 256–262.

16. Ibid., 165–185.

17. Nicoletta Misler, "Designing Gestures in the Laboratory of Dance," in Baer, *Theatre in Revolution*, 157–173.

18. Dobrovolskaya, *Lopukhov*, 143–155.

19. Souritz, *Soviet Choreographers*, 286. See also her essay "The Young Balanchine in Russia," *Ballet Review* 18, no. 2 (summer 1990): 67–68.

20. Souritz, *Soviet Choreographers*, 318, quoting from Lopukhov, *Sixty Years*, 257, 258. The Blue Blouse and TRAM (acronym for Theater of Working Youth) were agitprop theater groups.

21. Elizabeth Souritz, "Constructivism and Dance," in Baer, *Theatre in Revolution*, 134, 140.

22. Quoted in Larry Sitsky, *Music of the Repressed Russian Avant-Garde, 1900–1929* (Westport, Conn.: Greenwood Press, 1994), 173.

23. Souritz, *Soviet Choreographers*, 301–315.

24. Solomon Volkov, *St. Petersburg: A Cultural History*, trans. Antonina W. Bouis (New York: Free Press, 1995), 305; Nina Alovert, "From St. Petersburg to Leningrad: Lopukhov's Legacy," *Dance Magazine*, March 1989, 43; Roslavleva, *Era of the Russian Ballet*, 206.

25. Personal communication from Roland John Wiley, 4 January 1999.

26. Joan R. Acocella, "The Reception of Diaghilev's Ballets Russes by Artists and Intellectuals in Paris and London, 1909–1914," Ph.D. diss., Rutgers University, 1984, 68.

27. Mikhail Kolesnikov, "The Russian Avant-Garde and the Theatre of the Artist," in Baer, *Theatre in Revolution*, 86.

28. Jean D'Udine, *L'Art et le geste* (Paris, 1910), xiii, xvii.

29. Victor Seroff, *The Real Isadora* (New York: Avon, 1971), 134; Isadora Duncan, *The Art of the Dance* (1928; rpt., New York: Theatre Arts Books, 1969), 90.

30. Lynn Garafola, "Dance, Film and the Ballets Russes," *Dance Research*, 16, no. 1 (summer 1998): 11–12. The first private teachers of Dalcroze's work in Russia were Nina Alexandrova in Moscow, beginning around 1909, and Theodore Appia in St. Petersburg, from 1912. Personal communications from Selma L. Odom and Mary Trofimov, 25 May and 22 June 1999, respectively. However, we know that actors at St. Petersburg's Antique Theater studied eurhythmics during the 1910–1911 season; see Spencer Golub, *Evreinov: The Theatre of Paradox and Transformation* (Ann Arbor: UMI Research Press, 1984), 127.

31. Quoted in Misler, "Designing Gestures," 161.

32. Lupokhov, *Sixty Years,* 245.

33. Fedor Lupokhov, "My Answer" (Moi otvet)," *Zhizn' iskusstva* 8, 21 February 1922, 3.

34. Lillian Loewenthal, *The Search for Isadora: The Legend and Legacy of Isadora Duncan* (Pennington, N.J.: Dance Horizons, 1993), 146.

35. Emile Jaques-Dalcroze, *Rhythm, Music and Education,* trans. Harold F. Rubinstein (London: Chatto and Windus, 1921), 150.

36. Selma L. Odom, "Wigman at Hellerau," *Ballet Review* 14, no. 2 (summer 1986): 46–47.

37. Souritz, *Soviet Choreographers,* 265, 272.

38. Michel Fokine, quoted in Joan Lawson, *A History of Ballet and Its Makers* (London: Dance Books, 1973), 100–101. It is interesting that Fokine's musical analysis is casual in a couple of instances. He refers to a repeat of the first sixteen bars of music with varied orchestration, but the music does not repeat at this point. This is undoubtedly a matter of shaky memory or simple carelessness, not a matter of Fokine missing an obvious aspect of the musical structure. He also refers inaccurately to the imperfect cadences at the end of each sixteen bars, at points when there are perfect, more complete cadences. This could indicate a lack of understanding of musical theory.

39. Lupokhov, *Sixty Years,* 243. Lopukhov does not refer to the fact that Fokine was influenced by Duncan's practice.

40. James Billington, *The Icon and the Axe: An Interpretive History of Russian Culture* (London: Weidenfeld and Nicolson, 1966), 477.

41. Boris Asafiev, "Annals of *The Sleeping Beauty.* Part II: The Music," trans. Debra Goldman, *Ballet Review* 5, no. 4 (1975–1976): 38. The original article on *The Sleeping Beauty* is in *Letters on Russian Opera and Ballet,* Weekly Monitor of the Petrograd Academic Theaters 5 (1922): 28–36. This article is included in Asafiev's *Selected Works* (Izbrannye Trudy) (Moscow: Academy of Sciences of the USSR, 1954), 2, 175–182. See also Roland John Wiley, *Tchaikovsky's Ballets* (Oxford: Clarendon Press, 1985), 64; Asafiev, *Symphonic Studies* (Simfonicheskiye etyudi) (Petrograd: State Philharmonia, 1922).

42. Lupokhov, *Sixty Years,* 337–338.

43. However, this theory counters Fokine's theories of expressivity, which proposed the centrality of subject matter, narrative, or situation. *Les Sylphides,* so often cited as an example by later choreographers who were concerned with formal principles, is hardly representative of Fokine.

44. André Levinson, *Ballet Old and New* (1918), trans. Susan Cook Summer (New York: Dance Horizons, 1982), 79; Akim Volynsky, "Don Quixote" (1923), trans. in Stanley Rabinowitz, "Against the Grain: Akim Volynskii and the Russian Ballet," *Dance Research* 14, no. 1 (summer 1996): 17–20.

45. Joan Acocella and Lynn Garafola, eds., in *André Levinson on Dance: Writings from Paris in the Twenties* (Middletown, Conn.: Wesleyan University Press, 1991), 4, 5, 18–19.

46. Bronislava Nijinska, "On Movement and the School of Movement," in

Nancy Van Norman Baer, *Bronislava Nijinska: A Dancer's Legacy* (San Francisco: Fine Arts Museums of San Francisco, 1986), 85–88.

47. Akim Volynsky, "The Nature of Classical Dance," unpublished translation by Stanley Rabinowitz of excerpts from *The Book of Ecstasies* (Kniga Likovanii) (1925). (I am very grateful to Professor Rabinowitz for allowing me access to his translation.) Akim Volynsky, "The Book of Exultation" (1925) ("Croisée and Effacée"), trans. Seymour Barofsky, *Dance Scope* 5, no. 2 (spring 1971): 31–35. However, Lopukhov disagrees with Volynsky on detail: he claims that the alignments croisé and effacé are in themselves not dynamic but static metaphors, that en dedans/en dehors are the dynamic metaphors (26).

48. Quoted in Souritz, *Soviet Choreographers*, 62.

49. Lupokhov, *Sixty Years*, 183.

50. Levinson, *Ballet Old and New*, 72–76.

51. Ibid., 73–74.

52. Volynsky, "Music" (1925), trans. in Rabinowitz, "The House that Petipa Built: Visions and Villains of Akim Volynskii," *Dance Research* 16, no. 1 (summer 1998): 58–59.

53. Quoted in Camilla Gray, *The Russian Experiment in Art 1863–1922*, rev. ed. by Marian Burleigh-Motley (London: Thames and Hudson, 1986), 219.

54. Quoted in Volkov, *St. Petersburg*, 278.

55. Lupokhov, *Sixty Years*, 243.

56. Roslavleva, *Era of the Russian Ballet*, 205–206.

57. Souritz, *Soviet Choreographers*, 98. Lunacharsky and Asafiev were among those who stimulated the Soviet obsession with Beethoven. Boris Schwarz, *Music and Musical Life in Soviet Russia* (Bloomington: Indiana University Press, 1983), 93. According to Dobrovolskaya (*Lopukhov*, 93), Lopukhov's choice of the Fourth Symphony was influenced by the latter, as well as by the French novelist Romain Rolland, an early Soviet sympathizer.

58. Personal communication from Elizabeth Souritz, 19 April 2000. Struve also helped Lopukhov with the libretto of *Firebird*.

59. These drawings were included in the original program and reprinted in *Sixty Years* after p. 208. They have been used as illustrations in the current text.

60. Souritz, *Soviet Choreographers*, 269.

61. Dobrovolskaya, *Lopukhov*, 98.

62. "Tribute to Lopukhov" (1986), videorecording housed in the Dance Collection, New York Public Library for the Performing Arts.

63. Robert Greskovic, "Lopukhov Work Is Shown at NYPL," *Dance Magazine*, June 1991, 16.

64. Lupokhov, *Sixty Years*, 244.

65. The use of musical titles conforms to Balanchine's later practice.

66. Souritz, *Soviet Choreographers*, 276. An example is Igor Belsky's ballet *The Leningrad Symphony*, choreographed in 1961.

67. Roland John Wiley, "Dances from Russia: An Introduction to the Sergejev Collection," *Harvard Library Bulletin* 24 (1976): 94–112. I would

like to thank the Harvard Theatre Collection for providing me with microfilm copies of the choreographic notations of Petipa works.

68. Ibid., 107.

69. Labanotation scores written in 1962 and 1976 clarify this Royal Ballet version, while indicating a hold on pointe and "pawing" or brushing notion of the working foot, rather than a plié after the second relevé. The 1962 score by Ann Hutchinson (Guest) is based on Merle Park's performance (New York: Dance Notation Bureau). The 1976 score by Lynne Weber, assisted by Rosemary Valaire, is based on Eleanor D'Antuono's performance in Mary Skeaping's 1976 production for American Ballet Theatre, which also used the Sergeyev staging (New York: Dance Notation Bureau). I am deeply indebted to Ann Hutchinson Guest for drawing my attention to these Labanotation scores at the Language of Dance Centre and for imparting her knowledge of Stepanov notation so that I could make comparisons between choreographic versions.

70. The performance viewed featured Svetlana Zakharova as Aurora, Kirov Ballet, 13 June 2000, Royal Opera House, London.

71. The videorecordings of Kirov productions of *The Sleeping Beauty* consulted for this study were the 1983 USSR Gosteleradio/National Video Corporation International Ltd. release directed by Elena Macheret and starring Irina Kolpakova as Aurora and the 1989 RM Arts/Société Radio Canada release directed by Bernard Picard, with Larissa Lezhnina in the same role.

72. It is interesting that Frederick Ashton does note this hemiola-style interruption of the waltz rhythm in his 1946 staging of the music for the Sadler's Wells Ballet, although his is a playful, by no means straightforward visualization of music and involves a witty anticipation. He introduces his hemiola steps earlier, and they cross the music's waltz rhythms on first appearance. On repeat, they achieve rhythmic harmony, resolution with the accompaniment, which now too produces a two-beat hemiola effect. The first step, for an inner group of dancers, occurs during the first section of the dance, a simple posé retiré devant and coupé, *1 2*, repeated closing in fifth position, *3 4*, and an entrechat trois derrière, *5 6*, allowing the complete step to be immediately repeated on the opposite side of the body (all accents are on the "up" movements, on pointe or in the air). The second step, moving on the diagonal in and out of stage center, starts step, coupé, fouetté, followed by two runs and then, step, assemblé, changement, the last three moves particularly accenting *1 2 3 4 5 6* (accents now down into the ground); see Stephanie Jordan, *Moving Music: Dialogues with Music in Twentieth-Century Ballet* (London: Dance Books, 2000), 228–230.

73. In the Stepanov notation and on the Kirov videorecordings, the steps are variants of the opening balancé step: a step across in fifth devant in plié followed by two steps on pointe in fifth (the notation) or all three of these steps on pointe (the videos).

74. Lopukhov, "Annals of *The Sleeping Beauty*. Part I: The Choreography," trans. Debra Goldman, *Ballet Review* 5, no. 4 (1975–1976): 25, 30; Lupokhov, *Choreographic Revelations,* chapter on *The Sleeping Beauty*.

75. Marian Smith, "'Poésie lyrique' and 'Chorégraphie' at the Opéra in the July Monarchy," *Cambridge Opera Journal* 4, no. 1 (1992): 18.

76. Roland John Wiley, "Ars Longa: An Imperial *Swan Lake* Is Heard Again," *Dancing Times,* September 1997, 1074.

77. Marian Smith observes a general tendency toward the erosion of the composer's authority with regard to stage directions in opera. This was the case by the mid-nineteenth century. "Not only had the establishment of repertory opera prevented the composer, for logistical reasons, from partaking in the staging of each new production of a work, but changing structural conventions in the music (and, of necessity, the conventional stage movements that went with them) were having precisely the same effect. These changes of circumstance posed a serious threat to the composer's traditional means of controlling what happened on stage." Smith, "The Livrets de Mise en Scène of Donizetti's Parisian Operas," in *L'Opera Teatrale di Gaetano Donizetti,* Proceedings of the 1992 International Conference on the Operas of Gaetano Donizetti, Bergamo, Italy (Comune di Bergamo, 1993), 376.

78. I am very grateful to Giannandrea Poesio for discussing this passage with me and for lending me a videorecording of his reconstruction presented at Roehampton Institute London, 1998.

79. For a reproduction and transcription of the Stepanov notation of the Waltz of the Snowflakes, see Wiley, *Tchaikovsky's Ballets,* 389–400. It is hard to judge quite what Lopukhov means by "figures which change after every 8 bars do not work for the whole of the 'waltz of the snowflakes'" because Tchaikovsky's Waltz does create a regular eight-bar framework. Possibly, Lopukhov wishes for a choreographic response to the changing phrase lengths suggested by shifts between down- and up-beat phrasing (e.g., between rhythmic counting *1* 2 3 and 2 3 *1*), at which points the anticipated eight-bar unit is either shortened or lengthened. Perhaps, too, he wanted a choreographic response to the syncopations in the score. These suggestions are in line with his thinking in *The Ballet Master and His Art.* Certainly, such niceties are not suggested in the Stepanov notation, which stresses simple waltz rhythm steps without upbeat (pas de basque, balancés) or running.

80. Lopukhov, "Annals of *The Sleeping Beauty.* Part I: The Choreography," 24.

81. Fedor Lopukhov, "Premiere of New Grigorovich *Swan Lake* at Bolshoi," *Dance News,* February 1970, 1.

82. Yuri Slonimsky, "Balanchine: The Early Years," trans. John Andrews, ed. Francis Mason, *Ballet Review* 5, no. 3 (1975–1976): 14.

83. Sandra Noll Hammond, "Windows into Romantic Ballet, Part II: Content and Structure of Solo Entrées from the Early Nineteenth Century," *Proceedings of the Twenty-First Annual Conference of the Society of Dance History Scholars* (1998): 48.

84. I am indebted to Jennifer Thorp for providing me with these baroque and Renaissance examples of variation structure. See, for instance, Raoul-Auger Feuillet's "Folies d'Espagne pour femme" in his *Receuil de Danses* (1700) and Louis Pécour's "Folies d'Espagne pour un homme" in Feuillet's *Receuil d'Entrées de ballet de M. Pécour* (1704); Ann Daye, "Skill and Invention in the Renaissance Ballroom," *Historical Dance* 11, no. 6 (1991): 13.

"THE BALLET MASTER AND THE SCORE"

1. Igor Glebov is the pseudonym of the eminent Russian musicologist, critic, and composer Boris Asafiev (1884–1949). He is an important figure in ballet for a number of reasons. He wrote an early book on Stravinsky (Boris Asafiev, *A Book about Stravinsky*, trans. Richard French [Ann Arbor: UMI Research Press, 1982]. This is a translation of Asafiev's *Kniga o Stravinskom*, published in Leningrad in 1929. He is also important for his writings on the Tchaikovsky ballets. The 1922 *Simfonicheskiye etyudi* (Symphonic Studies), published in Petrograd, included articles on *The Sleeping Beauty* and *The Nutcracker*, which he saw as examples of symphonic ballet scores. The same year he published an article on *The Sleeping Beauty* in *Letters on Russian Opera and Ballet*, Petrograd Academic Theaters 5 (1922): 28–36. This article is included in Asafiev's *Selected Works* (Moscow: Academy of Science of the USSR, 1954), 2, 175–182, and it is translated by Debra Goldman, "Annals of 'The Sleeping Beauty.' Part II: The Music," *Ballet Review* 5, no. 4 (1975–1976): 36–43. Asafiev started work as a ballet pianist at the Maryinsky in 1910, later becoming a musical consultant there and a composer of twenty-eight ballet scores, the most famous of these being *The Fountain of Bakhchisarai* (1934) and *The Prisoner of the Caucasus* (1938). It is hardly surprising that Lopukhov added this note on the Glebov publication to his treatise, much of which he claims to have written in 1916. Asafiev was an important supporter during the early years of Lopukhov's directorship at the Petrograd State Theater.

Presumably referring to *The Sleeping Beauty*, Lopukhov cites 1889 as the date when a Russian first demonstrated the worth of writing music for ballet. He appears not to know that *Swan Lake* had already been produced in Moscow (1877, but 1894–1895 in St. Petersburg). Later, he refers to Tchaikovsky's *Swan Lake* as the composer's third ballet; it was the third to be seen in St. Petersburg. In fact, Tchaikovsky started work on *The Sleeping Beauty* in 1888, and the premiere was 3 January 1890. For a discussion of these works see Roland John Wiley's seminal volume *Tchaikovsky's Ballets* (Oxford: Clarendon Press, 1985).

2. Ivan Alexandrovich Vsevolozhsky (1835–1909) was the director of the Imperial Theaters from 1883 to 1899.

3. Lopukhov mentions the names of several "home-grown writers of tunes" of his day during the course of his treatise—Cesare Pugni (1802–1870), Ludwig Minkus (1827–1890), and Nikolai Sergeyevich Krotkov (b. 1849). The substitution technique is part of a long tradition in ballet of "impure" musical scores, large-scale borrowings from existing scores, variations taken from earlier ballets or specially written to suit a new ballerina in a role. Lopukhov mentions an example on p. 000, a variation from the ballet *Pygmalion* (see "Dance Symphonism," note 6).

4. *Ruslan and Ludmila* (1842).

5. In fact, the incidental ballet music in Rimsky-Korsakov's *Mlada* (1892) was written by Minkus. The work was conceived originally as a collaboration

between the Russian nationalist composers Mussorgsky, Cui, Rimsky-Korsakov, and Borodin, with Minkus providing the ballet music (Wiley, *Tchaikovsky's Ballets*, 9). Rimsky-Korsakov himself wrote disparagingly of his *Mlada* experience of ballet and remained highly prejudiced against the art form. See Nikolai Andreyevich Rimsky-Korsakov, *My Musical Life*, trans. Judah A. Joffe, ed. with introd. Carl Van Vechten (London: Eulenberg Books, 1974), 321; Nikolai Rimsky-Korsakov, letter to the critic Semyon Kruglikov, 2 February 1900, trans. in Richard Taruskin, *Stravinsky and the Russian Traditions: A Biography of the Works through Mavra* (Berkeley: University of California Press), vol. 1, 537.

6. The répétiteur is commonly used as the term for the violin rehearsal score.

7. Mention of the "trio" accompaniment to rehearsals probably means that the piano played the role of texturally filling out the musical score written in the form of a two-violin répétiteur. According to Lopukhov, this trio accompaniment became defunct in Fokine's day. However, according to Wiley (personal communication with author, 4 January 1999), even two-violin répétiteurs of pieces originally composed for piano survive, and for the Fokine repertory as well. The piano then came into its own as a sole accompanying instrument with the potential to reflect something of the orchestral sound, a more complex sound than that of conventional nineteenth-century ballet scores. Later in this chapter, Lopukhov writes of this potential of the piano, although he advocates saving time and achieving a more accurate sense of orchestration through direct study of the orchestral score. According to Lopukhov, in the late nineteenth century, the ballet composer would start the writing process with the répétiteur, which he or some other person would then orchestrate. This is most likely an incorrect account; the procedure makes little sense musically (confirmed by Wiley in a personal communication, 4 January 1999). It is the opposite of Tchaikovsky's procedure for *Swan Lake* and *The Sleeping Beauty*, when the full score was written first by Tchaikovsky, and then the répétiteur by someone else. Wiley tells us that the latter was the normal procedure at the time, though occasionally it was reversed (*Tchaikovsky's Ballets*, 4). Earlier practice in France was likewise to write the full score first: Adam created full score sketches for *Giselle* (1841) before writing the répétiteur.

8. The literal translation of this passage refers to "unisonal" orchestral performance of ballet music, which surely means not so much a strict unison pitch effect but rather the simplest single melody-accompaniment texture, as was provided by the rehearsal trio.

9. Vladimir Arkadievich Telyakovsky (1861–1924) became director of the Moscow Imperial Theaters in 1898 and then of the Imperial Theaters both in Moscow and St. Petersburg in 1901. He held this position until 1917.

10. *La Bayadère* (Petipa/Minkus, 1877). Asafiev reorchestrated the score in 1916.

11. Nicholas Grigorievich Sergeyev (1876–1951) was régisseur of the Imperial Ballet in St. Petersburg from 1903 to 1918, when he left Russia. It was Sergeyev who brought the notated scores of many Russian ballets to the

West, providing, for instance, the classical backbone of the repertory of what is now the Royal Ballet. The scores in Stepanov notation are in the Harvard Theatre Collection. Alexander Monakhov (1884–1945) was a dancer and, later, ballet master and teacher, first at the Maryinsky/Kirov Theater (from 1902 to 1931), then at the Bolshoi Theater (from 1931 to 1945).

12. The editing and reorchestration of the 1895 St. Petersburg production of *Swan Lake* are discussed by Wiley in *Tchaikovsky's Ballets*, 249–257. The work was carried out by the ballet conductor and composer Riccardo Drigo after Tchaikovsky's death. There is no evidence of Tchaikovsky's reactions to the first treatment of his score, by Julius Reisinger, in Moscow, in 1877, and, with no performance score or répétiteur extant, no certainty as to the extent of the modifications to the score on this occasion (ibid., 41–46). There is even less information available about the second Moscow version of *Swan Lake*, choreographed by Joseph Peter Hansen in 1882.

13. Lopukhov had an interest, of course, in "cleaning up" *The Sleeping Beauty*, which he did in his own 1922 production. Having consulted the primary sources on the ballet, he was correct in noting these amendments to Tchaikovsky's score. However, the new variation for Aurora in Act II (replacing Tchaikovsky's original variation) was in fact the original variation for the Gold Fairy in Act III; Cinderella had a new pas de deux for herself and Prince Fortuné (ibid., 153–154). Lopukhov's suggestion that Tchaikovsky was unhappy about making these adjustments and "following orders" conflicts with Wiley's account of Petipa's efforts toward a good collaboration in the attention he paid to Tchaikovsky with instructions, meetings to arrange details, and a solicitous if not reverential attitude toward changes in the score (155).

14. Lopukhov refers to Aurora's companions in this Act (Act II) as Nereids (sea nymphs). He does so again in the chapter on *The Sleeping Beauty* in his *Choreographic Revelations*, though here he mentions that sometimes they are Dryads (or wood nymphs), as in the Kirov production staged by Konstantin Sergeyev in 1951, when Simon Virsaladze (1909–1989) set the scene in an autumn forest. See "Annals of *The Sleeping Beauty*. Part 1: The Choreography," trans. Debra Goldman, *Ballet Review* 5, no. 4 (1975–1976): 31–32. Petipa's scenarios and the published libretto refer simply to Aurora's companions or friends (Wiley, *Tchaikovsky's Ballets*, 331, 367) and to their being discovered in cliff scenery and beside a river (not on a seashore).

15. *Les Caprices du Papillon* (Petipa/Krotkov, 1889).

16. The choreography of *The Nutcracker* (1892) is now attributed to Lev Ivanov (using Petipa's libretto after E. T. A. Hoffmann). Reports at the time of the creation of the ballet suggest, to varying degrees, Petipa's hand in the actual staging of the ballet, which might account for Lopukhov's reference to "joint staging." See Roland John Wiley, *The Life and Ballets of Lev Ivanov* (Oxford: Clarendon Press, 1997), 136–137.

17. Wiley maintains that Petipa's illness was the reason that Ivanov was assigned to choreograph *The Nutcracker*. However, he does suggest that Petipa's indisposition might have been partly a result of the difficulties this music posed for him (*Tchaikovsky's Ballets*, 200, 202). There is no evidence to suggest that Pepita had experienced any difficulty with the *Beauty* score

that might have prompted him to share choreographic duties with Ivanov on future Tchaikovsky ballets. In the case of *Swan Lake,* there is again no evidence to support Lopukhov's contention. In fact, Petipa's memoirs suggest that he relished the idea of setting the ballet. In any event, Ivanov began by setting Act II first and he did this completely independently of Petipa (Wiley, *Tchaikovsky's Ballets,* 244).

18. "Petipa's favorite tones" refers to the white acts in these ballets. Lopukhov is incorrect in saying that Act II was choreographed by Petipa (or jointly by Petipa and Ivanov, as he says later). Elsewhere, indeed, he himself noted (recalling comments by Alexander Shiryaev) that both Acts II and IV were choreographed by Ivanov, which is the current, widely held view. See Marius Petipa, *Materialy, vospominaniya, stat'i* (Materials, Recollections, Articles), ed. Yuri Slonimsky et al. (Leningrad: Leningrad State Theater Museum, 1971), 210.

19. It can be presumed that Lopukhov means the traditional pair of violins with piano accompaniment.

"THE DANCE SYMPHONY"

1. The article to which Lopukhov refers is his "Moi otvet" (My Answer), *Zhizn' iskusstva* (The Life of Art), 21 February 1922, 3.

2. The critic Akim Volynsky was an important ballet theorist of his time, writing for *Birzhevye vedomosti* (Stock Exchange News) (1911–1917) and *Zhizn' iskusstva* (The Life of Art) until 1924. He was highly disparaging of Lopukhov and his choreography in the early 1920s because of the modernism of his choreography and because of personal ill-feeling: Volynsky was an ardent supporter of Nicolas Legat for the directorship of the Maryinsky ballet, the post offered instead to Lopukhov. It is interesting that Lopukhov betrays none of this ill will either here or later; he was clearly prepared to admit his admiration for this critic's aesthetic views. Volynsky frequently made references to links between classical ballet and the organic, natural world. See the translated excerpts in Stanley J. Rabinowitz, "Against the Grain: Akim Volynskii and the Russian Ballet," *Dance Research* 14, no. 1 (summer 1996): 6, 14 (from Volynsky's 1925 *Kniga Likovanii* [translated as *The Book of Ecstasies* or *The Book of Exultation*]). The essay "The Nature of Classical Dance," from *The Book of Ecstasies,* focuses on this topic. I am grateful to Professor Rabinowitz for providing me with a translation of this essay (as yet unpublished).

"DANCE SYMPHONISM"

1. Lopukhov is perhaps referring to Boris Asafiev (Igor Glebov) as a force toward symphonization in dance, though the notion might also have stemmed from Duncan and Dalcroze tradition.

2. The use of symphonic poems "over the past five to seven years" suggests that this section of the treatise was written ca. 1916. Lopukhov would have been referring to Fokine's *Les Préludes* (Liszt, 1913), which he mentions later and would have seen, and perhaps to Fokine's *Schéhérazade* (Rimsky-Korsakov, 1910), which he might have seen in Paris in 1910.

3. Lopukhov appears to borrow the concepts of theme and thematic development from music to apply them to the deployment of movement material, motifs, and their development in dance.

4. This statement is completely at odds with Lopukhov's reflections on the symphonism in *Giselle, Swan Lake,* and *The Sleeping Beauty* later in this chapter.

5. Lopukhov refers here to pas de bourrée couru. The "little rope" step is a common step in Slavonic dance, a movement backward or forward, in which the foot of the working leg is raised with a shifting, brushing motion upward and along the higher part of the ankle/lower part of the calf before passing behind or in front of the supporting leg. The pattern formed is a rope or plait. I am indebted to Giannandrea Poesio for this information, gleaned from his interviews with Irina Gensler (a former dancer with the Kirov Ballet and teacher of character dance at the Vaganova Academy) and Sergei Vikharev (principal dancer with the Kirov Ballet), St. Petersburg, 9 October 1998.

6. *Pygmalion, or The Cyprus Statue* (Petipa/Prince Trubetskoy, 1883). *Le Corsaire* (Adam and Pugni) was originally choreographed by Joseph Mazilier in 1856, staged by Petipa in 1863, undergoing a number of revivals with additional choreography inserted, and music by Léo Delibes for the "Jardin Animé" scene (1868), the last revival involving Petipa in 1899. See *The Diaries of Marius Petipa,* ed., trans., and introd. Lynn Garafola, *Studies in Dance History* 3, no. 1 (spring 1992): 82.

7. Presumably Lopukhov here refers to the standard series of fouetté turns.

8. The arms (the port de bras motif) are characteristically crossed over the breast. Lopukhov's occasional misspellings of French terms, e.g., "sauté de basque," have been silently corrected.

9. See "The Ballet Master and the Score," note 19.

10. *Orfeo* is *Orpheus and Eurydice,* the 1911 Meyerhold production for which Fokine choreographed the dances, scenes, and groups. The *Polovtsian Dances* were choreographed for Act II of the 1909 production of Borodin's *Prince Igor.* When Lopukhov refers to Fokine's early works, he must be referring to the very early ones, for Fokine's first known choreography dates from 1905, and further down the page Lopukhov notes the presence of thematic choreographic development in his *Chopiniana* (1908), the version of the work that we know today. For some reason, Lopukhov does not mention Fokine's later, larger-scale ballets seen in Russia before the choreographer left there for good in 1918—*Francesca di Rimini* and *Eros* (both to Tchaikovsky in 1915), *Stenka Razin* (Glazunov, 1915), *Jota Aragonesa* (Glinka, 1916), and *The Sorcerer's Apprentice* (Dukas, 1916). Even though he was on military service in 1914–1916, Lopukhov made intermittent visits to St. Petersburg and saw the new Fokine ballets (Fedor Lopukhov, *Sixty Years in Ballet*

[Shestdesiat let v balete] [Moscow: Iskusstvo, 1966], 243). For a chronology of Fokine's ballets until 1917, see Lynn Garafola, *Diaghilev's Ballets Russes* (New York: Oxford University Press, 1989), 379–392.

11. Lopukhov's ideas about thematic choreographic development, the counteraction, conflict, and conjunction of choreographic themes, again suggest musical models, such as the sonata form, with its contrasting subjects or musical material. Lopukhov might also have noted here as models for thematic choreographic development the Shades scene from Petipa's *La Bayadère* (see the essay on the "Kingdom of the Shades" elsewhere in this volume) or indeed the theme and variations section danced by Swanilda's eight friends in the first act of *Coppélia* (Petipa after Arthur St. Léon/Delibes, 1884).

"THE POSITION OF DANCE IN RELATION TO MUSIC: SEPARATE, DOMINANT, SUBORDINATE, AND INTEGRATED"

1. Lopukhov suggests that the idea of integrating music and dance "as one" was "first put forward less than five years ago," which suggests that this part of the book was written around 1916. He is probably referring to the burgeoning of Dalcroze activity in 1912 and to the thinking of the Dalcroze propagandist Prince Sergei Mikhailovich Volkonsky in *Chelovek na stsene* (Man on the Stage) and *Khudozhestvennye otliki* (Artistic Responses), both published in St. Petersburg in 1912. Volkonsky was director of the Imperial Theaters from 1899 to 1901.

2. Strong and weak beats occur in music and dance as beats are clustered in twos or threes, the first beat of each cluster stressed or strong, the others weak. There are either two or three beats per bar, or a larger number of beats per bar clustered in twos or threes.

3. It is surprising that Lopukhov considers folk dance indifferent to the essential character of the music that accompanied it. He admits that there is bar by bar correspondence, but perhaps, given his particular theory of musical/choreographic relationships, he feels that folk dance does not correspond tightly enough to the melodic contour and note pattern rhythm of the music.

4. I interpret Lopukhov as using the term "rhythm" loosely here to mean "meter," even though he refers to the confusion between the terms earlier in this chapter.

5. Lopukhov appears to be referring to the Danse des Coupes.

6. It is a musical convention of long standing to read major and minor tonalities in particular ways, with major being associated with the positive, expressive qualities of, say, brightness and happiness, minor with darker qualities such as melancholy or sorrow.

7. *The Daughter of Pharaoh* (Petipa/Pugni, 1862).

8. Lopukhov clarifies here his impression that ballet masters and dancers up to and including Petipa did not uphold a close correspondence between

mime and music. The ballet masters lacked creative ideas, and the dancers indulged in "mime-improvisation." This resonates with Lopukhov's later reservations about the relationship between the Carabosse mime and its music (p. 000). But we know now that the correspondence between mime and music in the earlier romantic ballet in Paris had been very close. See Marian Smith, *Ballet and Opera in the Age of "Giselle"* (Princeton: Princeton University Press, 2000).

9. At various points in music history, different keys have been thought to possess different symbolisms, although, significantly, the symbols and the meanings of individual keys have shifted over the years.

10. *Giselle* (Petipa after Coralli and Perrot/Adam, 1884). The dance to which Lopukhov refers is a short solo within a group dance. In the original 1841 Paris production, this was the solo of the Spanish wili.

11. "Vortical" refers to the rotating, whirling round (as in a vortex) of the chaîné movement.

12. Lopukhov's term "motif" has been translated here as "phrase" to avoid the connotations of repetition by the term motif and to emphasize his primary meaning of a unit in time.

13. Here, with the end of the melody, Lopukhov's preoccupation is again with the time unit of the phrase, the end of the phrase being defined by melody (and harmony).

14. See the discussion of this variation in the introductory essay.

15. A cadence in music is a point of punctuation, the particular "perfect" type of cadence used in Albrecht's variation in bars 8, 16, and 24 being like a period at the end of a sentence. The single modulation in this variation occurs in bar 8, with a cadence to B-flat major. Immediately after this Adam returns to the home key of E-flat major.

16. The three sections or parts of this variation are bars 1–8, 9–16, and 17–24. Musical examples 10 and 11 together show all three sections.

17. The point about the entrechat-six landing on the high point of the melody (as if in opposition to the melody) raises the issue that jumps in Petipa style usually land on the musical accent. Here the jump lands on the second downbeat of the bar (in $\frac{6}{8}$ time, the beginning of the three-beat cluster halfway through the bar—see note 2, this chapter, which, as Lopukhov indicates, coincides with the moment of upturn in the melody.

18. Clearly, energy is seen as an important connecting parameter here between music and dance, not only rhythm and melodic contour. This is further confirmed in the explanation of musical example 11.

19. Lopukhov uses the term "melody" here to indicate a time unit, rather than a form of pitch organization.

20. See "The Ballet Master and the Score," note 1.

21. Adam's *Giselle* is an obvious example of a ballet in which musical motifs are associated with particular characters. Léo Delibes also introduced musical themes associated with specific characters in his ballet scores.

22. *La Fille Mal Gardée* (Ivanov and Petipa/Hertel, 1885). The ballet was first choreographed by Jean Dauberval in 1789.

23. There are leitmotifs associated with Carabosse and the Lilac Fairy.

However, Lopukhov is incorrect in his judgment, repeated on page 000, that all characters in *The Sleeping Beauty* are associated with musical leitmotifs.

24. The key shifts suddenly from F major to A major.

25. The fairies' entrance is clearly marked off from the previous march as a "Scène dansante."

26. The literal translation is "bar rhythm" or "rhythm of the bars." This has been translated as "meter" because all the evidence points to the fact that matching the detail of the note rhythm within the bar is an ideal that is not realized.

27. In the original ballet master's plan and published libretto, Carabosse entered in a wheelbarrow (Wiley, *Tchaikovsky's Ballets*, 361).

28. At bar 48 (which corresponds to the third bar of Lopukhov's musical example), the direction in Tchaikovsky's score reads "Le Roi et la Reine la supplient." This is the only direction until nine bars later, when Catalabutte throws himself at the feet of Carabosse. Presumably, Lopukhov would have seen these score directions as well as hearing the action from the music. See the discussion of this passage in the introductory essay.

29. The four mime artists referred to are Enrico Cecchetti (1850–1928), the famous dancer and ballet master, and the dancers Alexander Viktorovich Shiryaev (1867–1941), Alexander Ivanovich Chekrygin (1884–1942), and Vasily Nikolaevich Stukolkin (1879–1916).

30. See the discussion of the waltz in the introductory essay.

31. According to Lopukhov, the first figure of the waltz melody spans thirty-four bars (bars 41–74 in the score). It includes the sixteen-bar opening tune and its repeat, the latter referred to as the second half of the first figure (and shown in musical example 17, bar 57 in the score). The second melody figure begins at bar 75.

32. There is a hemiola effect here as the melody in half-notes strides across the $\frac{3}{4}$ meter. However, the accompaniment rhythm retains the $\frac{3}{4}$ meter, which Petipa chooses to follow choreographically. Lopukhov's view that relaxed, adjustment steps such as balancés would suit bars 15 and 16 is apt: this is after all a point of cadence, before a long "upbeat" to the second melody figure in the next two bars. Lopukhov suggests that Petipa's practice is to show a step unit four times, whatever the music.

33. Musical example 18 is a direct continuation of the music in musical example 17 and shows the second melody figure in the waltz.

34. Examples of six-bar musical units are bars 103–108 and 139–144.

35. *The Little Humpbacked Horse* (Petipa/Pugni, 1895). This ballet was first choreographed by Arthur St. Léon in 1864.

36. The implication here is that ballet composers adapted to the needs of ballet masters in the era of "dance to the accompaniment of music," a process that engendered an improved rapport between music and dance. Lopukhov clarifies later that the inexperienced Tchaikovsky would not have known how to do this; thus, his ballets suffer in their rapport between music and dance. In fact, Tchaikovsky borrowed extensively from existing ballet music stylistic traditions (Wiley, *Tchaikovsky's Ballets*, 40, 64). Wiley notes that Petipa's original instructions to the composer for *The Sleeping Beauty* were not especially

helpful or detailed, that Tchaikovsky responded freely to them, but that the two conferred when it came to making changes in the music (ibid., 109–111; see also "The Ballet Master and the Score," note 13). The method of collaboration was different from that between Petipa and previous specialist ballet composers, but Lopukhov's exaggerated statement suggests a lack of understanding between composer and choreographer that was not the case.

37. *Les Caprices du Papillon* was first performed at a gala on 5 June 1889 and given its first public performance on 25 October 1889. *The Sleeping Beauty* received its premiere on 3 January 1890.

38. See note 23, this chapter.

39. This is something of a misunderstanding of the Dalcroze eurhythmics system in which correspondences in movement that are not only of a rhythmic nature are theorized. For further discussion of Dalcroze, see the introductory essay.

40. Lopukhov uses the term artist to refer to both choreographers and dancers.

41. This folktale, which is a part of popular mythology in Russia, is a metaphor for boasting recklessly about achieving the impossible (personal communication from Elizabeth Souritz, 19 April 2000).

42. The original Russian reads: "within the category of the 'hard plié'—that is to say character dance." This has been translated here as "within the sphere of character dance." The categories of hard and soft plié are discussed in Lopukhov's chapter "The 'Soft' versus the 'Hard' Plié." "Hard" is likened to second-class travel (and used to refer to character dance), "soft" to first-class travel (and used for classical dance).

43. At this point Lopukhov might be referring to the work of the Moscow choreographer Kasian Yaroslavich Goleizovsky (1892–1970), a former Bolshoi dancer who spoke out against the traditional academic ballet of his day and formed his own experimental studio and company, the Moscow Chamber Ballet. He favored contemporary music, especially that of Scriabin, but one of his most significant works was *Faun* (1922), set to Debussy's *Prélude à l'après-midi d'un faune*. To heated response, the Chamber Ballet performed in Petrograd in autumn 1922. The program included *Faun*. This could be the use of Debussy to which Lopukhov refers. Although experimental, many see Goleizovsky as working fundamentally within classical tradition (Elizabeth Souritz, *Soviet Choreographers in the 1920s*, trans. Lynn Visson, ed. with additional trans. Sally Banes [Durham: Duke University Press, 1990], 154–215). The young Balanchine's enthusiasm for the choreographer is well known.

44. Lopukhov's comment on the lack of connection across the structures of music and dance in Albrecht's variation needs qualifying. There is a degree of connection in the musical structure. Even if there is no intertwining and development of themes to create an organic structure, there is simple repetition at a distance in the form of recapitulation.

45. The dance referred to here is Aurora's Act III variation in *The Sleeping Beauty*. See the discussion of this passage in the introductory essay.

46. A literal translation here is "reversed fifth position."

47. An example is the coda of the Black Swan pas de deux in *Swan Lake*,

set in $\frac{2}{4}$ (Allegro molto vivace) and featuring the male dancer in a grande pirouette.

48. *Carnaval* (Schumann, 1910). The pirouette occurs during the closing bars of Harlequin's solo to the presto "Paganini" movement.

49. See Volynsky, "The Book of Exultation ('Croisé and Effacé')," trans. Seymour Barofsky, *Dance Scope* 5, no. 2 (spring 1971): 31–35.

50. The Lilac Fairy enters in the Prologue, not Act I, of *The Sleeping Beauty*.

"CONCLUSION"

1. Dance critics continued to play a role in Soviet Russia: the point here is Lopukhov's lack of respect for their judgments. There is no mention here of the critic André Levinson, who had much in common with Volynsky in terms of aesthetic preferences (see the introductory essay). He had reviewed dance for *Rech'* and *Apollon* prior to the Revolution and for *Zhizn' iskusstva* between 1918 and 1920. However, Levinson had left Russia in 1921, clearly at odds with the Soviet regime, and it would likely not have been politic for Lopukhov to have mentioned his name here. In *Sixty Years in Ballet* (183), Lopukhov recognizes Levinson as a thoughtful, serious critic, while admitting that he did not agree with him consistently.

2. Lopukhov discusses the "grotesque" stage of choreographic development in part 1, chapter 4 of the treatise, referring to it as embracing elements of all choreographic ideas to date and requiring a new body shape and new movements. The discussion of the "soft" and "hard" plié occurs in the chapter "The 'Soft' versus the 'Hard' Plié." (See also "The Position of Dance in Relation to Music," note 42.)

3. Lopukhov refers here to professional dance schools that are attached to theaters.

4. Agrippina Vaganova (1879–1951), the celebrated Soviet teacher, established, with Nicolas Legat and Volynsky, a separate school of Russian ballet in Petrograd (1921–1925).

5. All of these are celebrated dancers: Virginia Zucchi (1849–1930), Pierina Legnani (1863–1923), and Evgenia Sokolova (1850–1925).

6. *The Snow Maiden* (1881, first performed 1882).

7. *Orfeo* (1911). See "Dance Symphonism," note 10.

"PETIPA AS CREATOR OF CHOREOGRAPHIC COMPOSITIONS IN SONATA FORM"

1. Lopukhov distinguishes the term "duet" from "pas de deux." In his previous chapter in *Choreographic Revelations*, "The Duet and the Pas de Deux," he maintains that duets reveal the personal relationship between the

characters and also serve to advance the story. Pas de deux, on the other hand, have no narrative function and develop in purely choreographic terms. Likewise, Lopukhov refers to the grand pas as an ensemble dance with a function similar to that of the duet, whereas the pas classique is its purely choreographic equivalent. Today, we are more inclined to use the term "grand pas" in Lopukhov's sense of the pas classique: a series of individual dance numbers for corps de ballet and soloists including pas de deux, adagio, coda, and sequence of solo variations, as in Petipa's *Paquita* (Minkus, 1881) and *Raymonda* (Glazunov, 1898). Note that in *Choreographic Revelations*, unlike *The Ballet Master and His Art*, Lopukhov transliterates French words such as pas de deux and ballet step terminology into Cyrillic. Thus, the translator here must also "translate" these terms.

2. This was probably Nadezhda Soboleva, who danced with Lopukhov in *The Parisian Market*, an 1859 Petipa ballet staged by Klaudia Kulichevskaya for the 1905 Student Workshop Performance (Bronislava Nijinska, *Early Memoirs*, trans. and ed. Irina Nijinska and Jean Rawlinson [New York: Holt, Rinehart and Winston, 1981], 140–141).

3. This was probably Zinaida Alekseevna Georgievskaia, who joined the Imperial Ballet in June 1900.

4. Alexander Viktorovich Shiryaev (1867–1941), dancer of the Imperial Ballet in St. Petersburg.

5. Nikolai Gustavovich Legat (1869–1937), known in the West as Nicolas Legat, dancer, ballet master, choreographer, and teacher.

6. The time signature is misleading. As written, the melody suggests $\frac{3}{4}$ rather than $\frac{6}{8}$. However, Lopukhov is clearly keen to demonstrate his ability to write musical notation.

7. See the introductory essay.

8. Tchaikovsky's *The Maid of Orleans* (1879), Act II, No. 10 in the score. There is no reference to any borrowing from André-Ernest-Modeste Grétry (1741–1813) in the 1880 Jurgenson vocal score.

9. Petipa choreographed *Giselle* after Jean Coralli and Jules Perrot in 1884. The music for this pas de deux is by Friedrich Burgmüller. The pirouette from a kneeling position has continued in the St. Petersburg ballet tradition.

10. Inserted into the ballet originally choreographed in 1846 at the Paris Opéra by Joseph Mazilier to music by Edward Delvedez.

11. The Maly production of *Paquita* dates from 1957 and was by Konstantin Boyarsky.

12. Tamara Karsavina (1885–1978), Lubov Egorova (1880–1972), Elsa Ivanovna Will (1882–1941).

13. *Esmeralda* (Pugni, 1886). Lynn Garafola has noted that the 1886 production is considered Petipa's definitive revision of the ballet, after Jules Perrot's original choreography of 1844, but she points out that "he had been tinkering with it since 1866." See *The Diaries of Marius Petipa*, ed., trans. and introd. Lynn Garafola, *Studies in Dance History* 3, no. 1 (spring 1992): 87. Vaganova staged the ballet at the Kirov Theater in 1935. The trio to which Lopukhov refers is presumably part of the pas de six interlude for which

Drigo wrote music (at Petipa's request), within the ball scene at the house of Fleur de Lys in Act III of the ballet. The pas de six also contained the Diana and Actaeon pas de deux that is still performed, in Vaganova's version, as a concert number today. According to classical myth, Diana, the goddess of hunting, was the patroness of chastity. She relented, taking the shepherd Endymion as her lover. However, she punished the intrusion of Actaeon by having him changed into a stag and torn to pieces by his dogs.

14. Georgy Georgievich Kiaksht (1873–1936); Leonid Sergeevich Leontiev (1885–1942); Vaslav Fomich Nijinsky (1889–1950); Anna Pavlova (1881–1931).

15. *The Daughter of Pharaoh* (Pugni, 1862).

16. Matilda Felixovna Kshesinskaya (1872–1971), known in the West as Mathilde Kchessinska.

17. Note that Petipa did not call *The Daughter of Pharaoh* a fairy-tale ballet. This is Lopukhov's description.

18. Sergei Nikolaevich Khudekov (1837–1927), ballet scenarist and historian.

19. Musical sonata form is in three sections, and the conventional organization is as follows: (1) exposition (containing a first subject in the tonic key and a second subject in the dominant key); (2) development (a reworking of exposition material); (3) recapitulation (a repetition of the exposition, with the second subject in the tonic key). The recapitulation is followed by a coda. Choreography can follow only the thematic aspects of this form, and it is unlikely that this pas de cinq does even this to any great extent. It cannot duplicate the harmonic structure that is the central aspect of sonata form.

20. *Raymonda* (Glazunov, 1898): this pas d'action is the dueling dialogue between Jean de Brienne and Abderakhman.

21. Pavel Andreyevich Gerdt (1844–1917), dancer and, later, teacher at the Imperial Ballet in St. Petersburg.

22. *Laurencia* (Chabukiani/Krein, 1939).

23. Yuri Slonimsky, *Didlo* (Didelot) (Moscow, 1956). Count Fedor P. Tolstoy, a naval school graduate, studied ballet with the choreographer Charles-Louis Didelot (1767–1837), became president of the Imperial Academy of Art, and created a set of ballet drawings now in the Russian Museum, St. Petersburg. See Mary Grace Swift, *A Loftier Flight: The Life and Accomplishments of Charles-Louis Didelot, Balletmaster* (Middletown, Conn.: Wesleyan University Press, 1974), 139.

24. Fokine's *Eros* (Tchaikovsky, 1915), *Les Sylphides* (or *Chopiniana*, Chopin, 1908), *Papillons* (Schumann, 1912).

25. Lev Ivanov's *Swan Lake* choreography (1894 and 1895); *Polovstian Dances* in *Prince Igor* (Borodin, 1890); czardas to Liszt's Second Hungarian Rhapsody, added to Charles Victor Arthur St. Léon's *The Little Humpbacked Horse* in 1900 (Pugni), later used in Gorsky's production of the same ballet (1901); *The Nutcracker* (1892); *The Enchanted Forest* (Drigo, 1887); *The Haarlem Tulip* (Fitinhof-Schell, 1887); *The Awakening of Flora* (Drigo, 1894); *The Mikado's Daughter* (Wrangel, 1897).

"THE CHOREOGRAPHY OF THE SHADES SCENE IN *LA BAYADÈRE*"

1. Valerian Yakovlevich Svetlov (1860–1934), writer on ballet.

2. Translator's note: In Russian the term "naturalism" is used to refer to an inferior kind of realism that aims to reproduce an "exact copy" of reality but is superficial in that it ignores underlying ideas.

3. Beethoven's Appassionata Sonata, op. 57 (1805).

4. *Don Quixote* (Petipa/Minkus, 1869).

5. Third position in the Russian school means both arms overhead.

6. Ravel's *Bolero* (1928).

7. This is surprising, given the technical difficulty of performing a smooth descent from arabesque on pointe into plié without support. In none of the productions of the ballet consulted for this essay (Kirov Ballet, Royal Ballet, and American Ballet Theatre) is the arabesque performed on pointe.

8. The pas de bourrée referred to here are pas de bourrée courus.

9. This bears an interesting relationship to the theory of Volynsky, certain details of which Lopukhov disagrees with in *The Ballet Master and His Art*. Volynsky proposed that effacé signifies calmness, whereas croisé implies pent-up tension. See "The Book of Exultation ('Croisé and Effacé')," trans. Seymour Barofsky, *Dance Scope* 5, no. 2 (spring 1971): 31–35. There is a greater emphasis on motion in Volynsky's descriptions than Lopukhov appears to accept in his treatise, where he considers these alignments as static metaphors in contrast with the dynamic metaphors of en dedans and en dehors (see p. 000). In *Choreographic Revelations,* Lopukhov seems to suggest a dynamic, motional potential in croisé that he denied in his early treatise.

10. Presumably, the petites sissonnes referred to here are the sissonnes ouvertes at the end of the waltz trio. The ballonnés are coupés-ballonnés performed by the corps de ballet on pointe and as jumps.

11. Nikiya performs two grands jetés entrelacés (en tournant) and then pas de bourrée courus to take her offstage.

12. The productions of the ballet consulted do not feature any jeté steps here.

13. In the productions consulted, the members of the corps support themselves on one arm while moving the other (described by Lopukhov later in this essay, referring to the recapitulation of ideas at the end of the scene).

14. There is surely no evidence of this link (although the arms are costumed in "oriental" style). The connection with ancient culture resonates with both Volynsky's and André Levinson's wish to relate classical ballet to Greek culture, thereby to validate it and to refute Duncan and others who appropriated ancient Greece for their brand of Greek dancing. Levinson refers to Maurice Emmanuel's comparison of dance depictions on vases and reliefs with photographic records of ballet, to demonstrate the kinship between ancient Greek dance and classical ballet. See Levinson, *Ballet Old and New* (1918), trans. Susan Cook Summer (New York: Dance Horizons, 1982), 66.

Volynsky maintains that the "entire essence and structure [of classical dance] have been bequeathed to us by the ancient world," in "Ballet" (1925), trans. in Stanley Rabinowitz, "The House That Petipa Built: Visions and Villains of Akim Volynskii," *Dance Research* 16, no. 1 (summer 1998): 56.

15. In the productions consulted the dancer performs cabriole, balancé, cabriole, balancé, as opposed to "four ordinary waltz balancés."

16. Marina Semenova, the first great Soviet ballerina (b. 1908).

17. The petite sissonne referred to here must be the sissonne simple of the Russian school that is a relevé to pointe on one leg, opening and closing in fifth position, with the working foot raised to the knee. The later note on "the sissonne that we have also seen before" is curious, for Lopukhov has just stated that the petite sissonne is a "new movement." In the productions consulted, there is no evidence of any other kind of sissonne in this variation.

18. In the productions consulted, the turn is in arabesque, not attitude.

19. Vasily Tikhomirov (1876–1956), dancer and teacher, trained at the Bolshoi School, spent most of his career with that company, becoming one of the most famous teachers of his time. Alexandre Volinin (1882–1955) and Fedor Kozlov (1882–1956) were other Bolshoi dancers.

20. Grand jeté entrelacé (en tournant): see note 11, this chapter.

21. The dancer performs pas de bourrée courus down the diagonal, halting twice to perform sissonnes simples (as described in note 17) to one supporting leg and then to the other.

22. He refers here to the pose of the statue of Mercury in Bologna, the attitude referred to by Carlo Blasis in *An Elementary Treatise upon the Theory and Practice of the Art of Dancing* (1820; repr., New York: Dover Publications, 1968), 36.

SELECTED BIBLIOGRAPHY

Alovert, Nina. "From St. Petersburg to Leningrad: Lopukhov's Legacy." *Dance Magazine*, March 1989, 42–46.

Asafiev, Boris. "Annals of *The Sleeping Beauty*. II. The Music." Trans. Debra Goldman. *Ballet Review* 5, no. 4 (1975–1976): 36–43.

Baer, Nancy Van Norman, ed. *Theatre in Revolution: Russian Avant-Garde Stage Design 1913–1935*. London: Thames and Hudson, 1991.

Balet Entsiklopediia (Ballet Encyclopedia). Moscow: Sovetskaia entsiklopediia, 1981.

Billington, James. *The Icon and the Axe: An Interpretive History of Russian Culture*. London: Weidenfeld and Nicolson, 1966.

Bowlt, John E. *The Silver Age: Russian Art of the Early Twentieth Century and the "World of Art" Group*. Newtonville, Mass.: Oriental Research Partners, 1979.

Devereux, Tony. "Legend of a Lost Choreographer." *The Dancing Times*, January 1998, 339–341 (pt. 1), and February 1998, 432–434 (pt. 2).

Devereux, Tony. "Lopukhov (Fedor)." *International Dictionary of Ballet*. Vol. 2. Detroit: St. James Press, 1993.

Dobrovolskaya, Galina. "Lopukhov, Fedor." *International Encyclopedia of Dance*. Vol. 4. New York: Oxford University Press, 1998.

Dobrovolskaya, Galina. *Fedor Lopukhov*. Moscow–Leningrad: Iskusstvo, 1976.

Fitzpatrick, Sheila, Alexander Rabinowitch, and Richard Stites, eds. *Russia in the Era of NEP: Explorations in Soviet Society and Culture*. Bloomington: Indiana University Press, 1991.

Gray, Camilla. *The Russian Experiment in Art 1863–1922*. Rev. ed. Marian Burleigh-Motley. London: Thames and Hudson, 1986.

Levinson, André. *Ballet Old and New* (1918). Trans. Susan Cook Summer. New York: Dance Horizons, 1982.

Levinson, André. *André Levinson on Dance: Writings from Paris in the Twenties*. Ed. and introd. Joan Acocella and Lynn Garafola. Hanover: UPNE/Wesleyan University Press, 1991.

Petipa, Marius. *The Diaries of Marius Petipa*. Ed., trans., and introd. Lynn Garafola. *Studies in Dance History* 3, no. 1 (spring 1992).

Rabinowitz, Stanley. "Against the Grain: Akim Volynskii and the Russian Ballet." *Dance Research* 14, no. 1 (summer 1996): 3–41.

Rabinowitz, Stanley. "The House That Petipa Built: Visions and Villains of Akim Volynskii." *Dance Research* 16, no. 1 (summer 1998): 26–66.

Roslavleva, Natalia. *Era of the Russian Ballet 1770–1965.* Foreword Ninette de Valois. London: Gollancz, 1966.

Schwarz, Boris. *Music and Musical Life in Soviet Russia.* Bloomington: Indiana University Press, 1983.

Sitsky, Larry. *Music of the Repressed Russian Avant-Garde, 1900–1929.* Westport, Conn.: Greenwood Press, 1994.

Souritz, Elizabeth. *Soviet Choreographers in the 1920s.* Trans. Lynn Visson. Ed. with additional trans. Sally Banes. Durham: Duke University Press, 1990.

Swift, Mary Grace. *The Art of the Dance in the USSR.* Notre Dame, Ind.: University of Notre Dame Press, 1968.

Volkov, Solomon. *St. Petersburg: A Cultural History.* Trans. Antonina W. Bouis. New York: Free Press, 1995.

Volynsky, Akim. "The Book of Exultation." Trans. Seymour Barofsky. *Dance Scope* 5, no. 2 (spring 1971): 16–35.

Wiley, Roland John. *Tchaikovsky's Ballets.* Oxford: Clarendon Press, 1985.

Wiley, Roland John. *The Life and Ballets of Lev Ivanov.* Oxford: Clarendon Press, 1997.

Yoffe, Lydia. "The Lopukhov Dynasty." *Dance Magazine,* January 1967, 35–39, 70–71.

SELECTED WRITINGS BY LOPUKHOV

Writings in Russian

Note: For a detailed list of Lopukhov's writings in Russian, see his *Sixty Years in Ballet,* 353–357.

The Ballet Master and His Art (Puti baletmeistera). Berlin: Petropolis, 1925.

Choreographic Revelations (Khoreograficheskie otkrovennosti). Moscow: Iskusstvo, 1972.

Sixty Years in Ballet (Shestdesiat let v balete). Moscow: Iskusstvo, 1966.

Writings in English

"Annals of *The Sleeping Beauty.* Part I: The Choreography." Trans. Debra Goldman. *Ballet Review* 5, no. 4 (1975–1976): 21–25. Translation of the essay on *The Sleeping Beauty* in *Choreographic Revelations.*

"Premiere of New Grigorovich *Swan Lake* at Bolshoi." *Dance News,* February 1970, 1, 17. Translation of an article published in *Izvestia,* 2 January 1970.

"Yuri Grigorovich's *Stone Flower:* His First Big Break." *Dance News,* July 1979, 1, 16. Translation of material from *Sixty Years in Ballet.*

Index

SOCIETY OF DANCE HISTORY SCHOLARS

The Society of Dance History Scholars is a not-for-profit organization dedicated to promoting study, research, discussion, performance, and publication in dance history and related fields. SDHS is a constituent member of the American Council of Learned Societies.